Any Fool Can Be a
Middle Aged Downshifter

by
Mike Woolnough

The Good Life Press LTD

ISBN 978 1 90487 1576
A catalogue record for this book is available from
the British Library.

Published by
The Good Life Press Ltd.
PO Box 536
Preston
PR2 9ZY

www.goodlifepress.co.uk
www.homefarmer.co.uk

Printed in the UK by Cromwell Press Group

This book is dedicated to Susie,
for putting up with me and my mad schemes and ideas for
over 30 years.

Mike Woolnough, Ipswich, 2009

Just call us Tom and Barbara

I wish I had a quid for every time somebody has said to me "We'll have to call you Tom and Barbara from now on then." It's funny how they all seem to think this is such an original joke too. I think everybody in the UK must have heard of, and probably seen, the TV series *The Good Life* where a married couple give up their jobs and run a smallholding in their back garden in suburban Surbiton, and as soon as anybody hears that we grow our own fruit and veg and have livestock they make the inevitable connection. It was quite funny for the first couple of hundred times, but after that it wore a bit thin.

People often say to me that I must have been inspired by John Seymour, the great self-sufficiency guru of the 1960s and 70s, but the truth is that in the early days I had never even heard of him. Like him though, I arrived in self-sufficiency by accident, and live on very little income, supplementing my meagre earnings with some writing. Friends reading my articles in magazines have said that I should write a book about our adventures, so............

Where do I begin? Well, some background would be a good start, I suppose!

I'm now in my mid-fifties and have never been a model employee. I have walked out of, or been fired from, more jobs than I care to remember – writing an honest CV for myself would be an almost impossible job as my memory really isn't good enough. One thing for sure is that I will never be awarded a gold watch for long service. It's not that I don't do a good job, more that I am extremely independent and once I know what my job is, I like to be left alone to get on with it. I am very much somebody who leads from the front, and I wouldn't expect somebody to do a job that I'm not prepared to do myself. Similarly I can't accept being told to do something I see as patently stupid or impractical.

I have always been happiest doing my own thing, and one of my most contented spells came to an end in August 2002, following the 9/11 attacks the previous year. In June 1993 I had opened a secondhand furniture shop, carrying out house clearances and selling the resulting antiques, household furniture, collectables.....and general junk. This was a highly enjoyable job as long as you didn't mind hard work and getting dirty - does this sound familiar to any smallholders reading this? As a life long compulsive collector I loved it, and was fascinated by the little treasures that I found over the years. Sadly the introduction of the electrical safety and soft furnishings fire regulations were the kiss of death for many secondhand shops. I found that I was taking more furniture and appliances to the corporation tip than I was selling, and so turned to selling new furniture. I found a source of three piece suites returned by catalogue companies, and business boomed. This led to retailing new three-piece suites and sofabeds, new bigger premises and an interesting looking future – until the attacks in America.

The effect was dramatic and disastrous for us. The great British public just stopped spending their money. Perhaps they thought that World War Three was about to start and so hung onto their cash, I really don't know, but retailers all over the country began to struggle, along with their suppliers and manufacturers. As a small independent shopkeeper I had no chance really, and ran up big debts trying to keep my business afloat. Eventually I just had to call it a day and close, and we were forced to sell our house and move to something smaller to clear up what we owed. When companies such as Alders and Courts went bust later, it made me feel slightly better – at least I knew my business hadn't folded through any bad management on my part.

So, after nearly ten years of doing my own thing I was suddenly thrown back into the world of being an employee, and it didn't sit well with me. After several short-lived jobs, a spell gardening for other people made me realise how much I enjoyed working outside, and my mind began to tick over........

We had been vegetarian for about three years. We had been dismayed by the disasters that had struck British meat farming: mad cow disease, swine fever and finally foot and mouth. We weren't worried about the effects on our health by eating meat, but more by the massive wasteful loss of life. My understanding is that foot and mouth is rarely fatal to the victim, it is a form of animal flu, but it *does* affect the animal's milk yield. So, millions of animals died on purely economic grounds, when the problem can be simply resolved by vaccination. Arguments against vaccination carry little weight with me – yes some effect would be felt on exports, but just look at the billions of pounds the FMD outbreak of 2001 cost the country's economy.

We were now beginning to hear some alarming stories about how supermarket vegetables were grown too. At this rate we would be starving, with no food to eat that we considered ethically edible. At least if we starved to death our bodies would be nicely embalmed by the numerous preservatives we had consumed in our lifetimes.

I fancied trying to grow some vegetables. This was a very ambitious plan for somebody whose only previous attempts had been some very scrawny tomato plants in a grow bag outside the back door. I thought that if I suggested digging up our newly landscaped and fenced back garden I may encounter a certain amount of resistance from she who must be obeyed, so I set out to get an allotment. We lived on one of the largest council housing estates in Europe and were lucky to have a very large allotment field just a couple of hundred yards from our front door.

Any Fool Can Be A......

The field secretary duly showed us around and offered a choice of two or three plots that were all totally choked solid with speargrass, and even I knew that this is one of the hardest weeds to clear. He could tell from the expressions on our faces that we were less than impressed with his offerings and so he ventured, "I think John may be giving up this plot as he has taken another one next to his original plot on the other side of the field," and indicated a plot that had a few motley vegetables growing in the midst of a jungle of weeds. We nearly bit his hand off as we urged him to find out for us. Well it turned out that John was indeed giving up on that plot for the convenience of two together, and so we inherited plot 85 on Aster Road Allotments.

I came to know those weeds very well. I am still battling with something that glories in the name of *Gallant Soldier*. It seems that it has earned its name from the fact that no matter how many times you knock the damned thing down it picks itself up and carries on growing! The story told on the 'lotty' is that it arrived eight years or so ago in a load of pig's muck and then rampaged across the field, and that it was originally an escapee from Kew Gardens. If that is the truth then Kew deserve to be severely chastised as it is one of the most tenacious weeds that I have come across – excepting bindweed, that is. The only plus point in its favour is that the chickens like it, although the goats aren't so keen.

There are a couple of points in that last sentence that might give you an indication of where we were headed.

I quickly set about clearing our miniature jungle and immediately began to wonder what I had let myself in for. It was fast approaching autumn and whilst there wasn't an urgency for clearing the whole plot, that would come in the spring, but we certainly needed to have some open ground to plant one or two winter crops. I learned the hard way that the only way to get rid of the weeds was to put in some hard graft and dig deep, picking out every scrap of perennial weed. Leave one tiny piece of root down there and magically you have a new plant appear. The soil was also full of *Gallant Soldier* and *Fat Hen* seeds. A week after I cleared a patch it would be covered in literally hundreds of tiny seedlings.

I very quickly discovered that the vegetable-growers best friend is his hoe – and a double edged one is best of all. Only after I had managed to decapitate most of our few inherited useful vegetables with my clumsy attempts did one of my neighbours show me his hoe. It was a German manufactured one with cutting edges to both sides so that you could use it with both pushing and pulling motions, and is much more controllable. My mother bought me one (they are expensive) and it proved to be the single most useful tool I have. The damage to our crops has decreased considerably since the new hoe arrived, and the weeds live much shorter lives too. I quickly discovered that the sooner you behead a weed, the better the chance that it will prove fatal, and a sunny dry day is better for hoeing than in wet conditions. It's ironic that an uprooted weed will quickly re-root itself given half a chance, but take a tiny slice out of one of your veg and it will keel over and die.

A couple of months after getting the allotment I decided that our own supply of fresh eggs would be a good idea, and I persuaded Sue that we should get a couple of hens. She was very dubious about it and spent hours scouring the contents of the local library reading up about chickens. The books were full of 'chook' diseases that very nearly put her off, but eventually she decided that she liked the look of Light Sussex, and their temperament seemed suitable.

The seeds had now been sown, and we were irretrievably lost. We were going mad....M.A.D....Middle Aged Downshifters.

Any Fool Can Be A.......

We set off into the wilds of deepest, darkest Norfolk to buy all the necessary bits and pieces, visiting a place that sold houses and runs as well as feeders, food and the essential Light Sussex. At first the lady owner tried to talk us into another breed as she had several varieties that were ready to go, but when we stuck to our guns wanting LS, she eventually took us to a run with several birds which were a little younger. We were treated to the sight of her chasing the selected birds around the run with a damn great fishing landing net, whilst we fought off the attentions of a very persistent Black Rock hen that decided she wanted to come home with us, even trying to get into our car with us. Black Rocks are tough birds that seem to cope with most things, so in light of what happened later perhaps we should have let her climb aboard.

The breeder eventually managed to catch a nice-looking Light Sussex but then held it to her ear and put it down again. The next two that she caught she brought out to us. When I asked why she decided against the first one she said that "It sounded a little chesty." Now this is the point where the experienced chicken keepers amongst you will be yelling "put them back" and tearing your hair out in frustration, but we were naïve beginners. We duly coughed up all the money that Sue had saved towards a new bed, and were the proud owners of a double-decker ark, a motley assortment of feeders, drinkers, straw and food….and two Light Sussex large fowl. This was all duly ensconced in a corner of our garden, and we settled down and waited to enjoy our first fresh egg. We had been told that they were 'point of lay' when we chose them, and so expected a nicely shelled offering any day. Some months later we learned that the term 'point of lay' means anything over 12 weeks old in chookspeak and these were probably younger than that, so we were in for a long wait as the actual age that most chickens start laying is around 20 weeks. In the meantime one of the pair had shown us that she was a very noisy talkative bird and so she was named *Moaning Myrtle* after the ghost in the girls' lavatories in the Harry Potter books. Her sister was named *Ginny* after Ron Weasley's sister....and so the naming theme for our chooks, and our love affair with Sussex chickens, began.

The first day we had a pantomime as dusk approached. The birds had been let out into the garden and became very agitated and wanted to find somewhere to roost, but being dumb chooks didn't realise that they were supposed to climb up the ramp to their bedroom. Despite our best efforts they were determined to settle down to sleep in a corner on the ground. When one nearly knocked itself out by trying to fly in through our kitchen window, Sue hit upon the idea of lighting their sleeping compartment and we placed a lit torch in the nestbox. Immediately one of them was craning its neck to see what was up there, and very quickly scrambled its way up the ramp.

The other one followed not long afterwards. Problem solved.

𝕿𝖍𝖊 𝕮𝖍𝖎𝖈𝖐𝖊𝖓 𝖍𝖆𝖘 𝖑𝖆𝖓𝖉𝖊𝖉

Any Fool Can Be A.......

But not quite. The next morning we could hear agitated noises coming from their roosting area. The stupid things were now too scared to climb *down* the ramp!

Opening the side door and shoving them down headfirst seemed to do the trick and in a couple of days they learned how to get up and down easily.

The birds, particularly *Myrtle*, didn't seem to grow very much despite our best loving care. We quickly decided that the area under the ark wasn't really big enough to keep the birds confined in, and that we had been sold something that wasn't really suitable for the purpose for which it had been bought, or the birds that we intended keeping in it. We started letting the birds out for a spell free ranging in the garden, and this eventually evolved into a permanent arrangement. We let them out first thing in the morning and shut them up again at dusk. Our garden is surrounded by a six foot fence so we considered them to be safe. The girls would spend most of the day sitting in the shade under a bush in our shrubbery.

Of course, like all chicken fanciers, we didn't stop there. We decided that as our ark could hold more, then of course we needed more chooks. We also fancied breeding them. Although we hadn't eaten meat for three years that wouldn't stop us eating it again. Meat that we knew the history of – exactly what had gone into it (or more precisely what *hadn't* gone in) would be perfectly acceptable. So *Hermione* and *Hagrid* joined the flock. Both of them were beautiful birds. We were also given the option of a full grown cockerel but he was a monster and scared the living daylights out of Sue, so we settled on a young lad. I suppose in the back of our minds we realised that he would grow, but we didn't worry about it. All four of them crammed themselves into the ark and settled down to marital bliss.

The next morning we were woken at 5.00am by some raucous screeching from the back garden. The sun was coming up. *Hagrid* was awake and letting the world know about it. Luckily we had neighbours either side who really weren't worried about the racket as they slept in the front bedrooms. It must have been a year later, after we had moved the birds, that we discovered that one neighbour to the rear of us had spent months waiting for Christmas to come. When Christmas passed and the crowing continued she hoped that he was going to be Easter dinner instead. She didn't know where the racket was coming from and so couldn't report us. High fences can be very useful.

After a few days *Hagrid* stopped crowing. Peace.

We were too inexperienced to realise that something was wrong. *Myrtle* meantime had actually got smaller rather than grown, and just moped around all day. She ate if I threw something tasty near her, but other than that she didn't seem interested. Eventually I was so concerned that I caught her up and examined her. She was a bag of bones with no meat on her whatsoever. She was obviously very ill and I decided to put her out of her misery. I had read the books and studied the diagrams of how to kill a bird, and so confidently did the deed.

But she didn't die. I hadn't got it right, and it was sickening to see her suffer.

In the end I smashed her head against a brick wall to finish her off quickly. I felt awful. This wasn't what we set out to do. When we started breeding we wanted our birds to have a good life and then die quickly and painlessly if we were going to eat them.

The next day I noticed that *Hagrid* was sitting hunched up and then stretching his neck and gaping. When I studied the others I realised that we had a problem.

Any Fool Can Be A......

We decided to take *Hagrid* to the vet. The vet examined him, and then we discovered that we had *Mycoplasma* in our flock, and that the first bird that was discarded by the breeder as being a 'bit chesty' was in fact very sick. We had bought unhealthy birds, and then introduced our beautiful new birds to their illness, and on reflection it is clear to me that the breeder knew she had a problem but didn't want to lose a three hundred quid sale for the sake of not being able to supply us with the breed of bird that we wanted. Cynical salesmanship.

The upshot was that we had to give all of them injections of antibiotics morning and night. We decided that *Ginny* was also too far gone, and so I had the unpleasant job of destroying her. It wasn't as bad as poor *Myrtle,* but was still very unpleasant. And so we began a ten day routine of giving the birds their twice-daily jabs. It sounds easy, but it was far from it. We had to get up while it was still dark and creep down the garden to grab them from their perches whilst they were still sleepy, cram them in boxes, and carry them to the dining room table for their shots. The needle had to be inserted into the muscle of the breast area, and they weren't exactly keen on it. We had to repeat this comedy in the evening too after the birds had roosted.

To her credit Sue was wonderful. She had a fear of birds, and all things flying, but would dutifully hold tight to one of the birds whilst I gave them their injections. All went well until one night I gave *Hagrid* his jab and must have hit a nerve. There was a God almighty squawk and *Hagrid* made a bolt for freedom with a hypodermic hanging out of his chest, dragging Sue across the table. She gamely hung on tight and I managed to get the needle out of him without breaking it.

The resulting vet's visit and medication cost us about thirty quid, nearly the price of the birds, and the pantomime with *Hagrid* taught us that roosters are very powerful lads.

We were now two birds short though so *Minerva* (Minnie) and *Sybill* came and joined us and the Harry Potter theme continued.

Having been sacked yet again from a fulltime job, I found myself a job for the winter, working in the offices of a local seed company. I worked three or four days a week, sitting there with my telephone headset on and taking orders from customers around the world and chatting about what they were growing and how they lived their lives. The company encouraged us to interact with the customers about their growing and I am a very chatty person, so the job suited me well and I found the lifestyles of some of the smallholders fascinating. The job was supposed to last from the beginning of September until the end of March, and I had calculated that by working more or less fulltime through the winter we could just about manage through the summer. We have no mortgage or rent to pay, the kids have all left home, and I don't drink (much), smoke or associate with bad women, so our needs are small.

Unfortunately business was bad and the company laid me off at the end of October with the promise of more work starting in January when it would get very busy. I duly reported back at the start of January – and was laid off again by the end of February! They told me that it had been an exceptionally bad year, but that if I came back in September, as a returnee I wouldn't be one of the first ones booted out next season.

Having not made as much money as I hoped during the winter, I realised that I wouldn't get through the summer, and so I found myself a permanent part-time job in the local supermarket. I worked one day a week from 1.00pm to 10.00pm, ironically in the produce department. It was hard physical work and I lost a lot of weight but it was flab that I could afford to lose and it gave me plenty of time to get the allotment up and running. I could bear being an employee by telling myself constantly that it allowed me to live the lifestyle that I was now seeking…..although of course we weren't going M.A.D.

I had now joined an internet forum called Alternative Country Lifestyles. ACL was populated with dreamers like myself, and a fair few people who were actually living the 'good life.' Over the years many had moved to Scotland or Wales in order to be able to buy the land to live their dream, and many more were now moving to France, Spain and even Canada as land prices here became out of reach.

Family commitments meant that we couldn't follow suit, but I read their posts and dreamed……………

We are full of beans.

That first autumn I had just cleared part of our plot when a sign appeared on the gate to the allotments: 'Aquadulce broad beans and Kelvedon Wonder peas available in the stock shed.'

I *hate* broad beans and made this observation to an old boy who was just coming in.

"Don't be so bluddy daft boy, them's so easy to grow, and if yew pick 'em young they're bootiful," he rebuked me.

My hatred stemmed from childhood memories of beans with skins so thick you could resole your shoes with them. Sue agreed with me, as this was how she remembered them too, and she didn't like them. We have never bought broad beans in the shops, so don't know if this is still the way they are sold these days.

Anyway, we had nothing much else planned to plant at that stage, so I decided to invest the princely sum of 80p in a bag of Aquadulce, and duly sowed them in early October. About three weeks later they had virtually all germinated and were showing a couple of leaves each. They grew to a few inches high before the bad weather arrived, and then hibernated for the winter.

It was very late in the season, but we managed to find some strawberry plants. Each pot had three or four runners on it so we had a bargain with buy one, get four free. They too were duly installed in a newly dug bed, and we looked forward to June.

I began work on building the Chicken Hilton on the allotment. We had inherited an old 8′ x 6′ shed on the plot and decided to partition part of it off for the chickens, and built a 15′ x 10′ attached run. Foxes are a big problem all over the allotments, so I knew I had to make it pretty much bombproof. The shed was standing on paving slabs, which was good, but it was rather rotten in some areas so I had to reinforce the sides to stop *Reynard* munching his way in. I built the run with three inch square wooden posts covered in chicken wire, and covered it over in more chicken wire stitched meticulously to the sides. The floor was excavated out, covered all over with chain link fencing laid flat and also stitched to the sides, and then re-covered with the soil. To date no fox has managed to get into this house or run, but I hope I'm not tempting fate by saying that.

The chicken bug was starting to bite and we had borrowed a small incubator and bought six Light Sussex eggs on Ebay, as our lot weren't old enough to start breeding from yet. Two proved to be infertile, and two had got scrambled in the post, but we spent a totally enthralled evening watching two little bundles of fluff emerge from their shells. I made a brooder from a plastic storage box and an anglepoise lamp fitted with a red bulb, and they thrived.

Any Fool Can Be A.......

By now we were in chicken overdrive, had bought a secondhand ark, again through Ebay, and spotted an advert for a trio of Buff Sussex in Hertfordshire. I duly galloped off on a five hour round trip to pick them up, and they were settled into the new ark in the garden. They and the Lights were let out on alternate days, but *Hagrid* wasn't very pleased and tried to kill *George* (Weasley), the new buff boy, through the wire every day. We decided to move *Hagrid* and one of the girls over to the new housing on the allotment, and all the rest were let out into the garden together.

They were a beautiful sight free ranging together in the garden, and each group returned to their own house at night......all except that little trollop *Hermione,* who decided that she wanted to sleep with *George!* She was turfed out three nights running when we shut them up and she eventually got the message.

We have a garden bench outside our dining room window and all the chooks thought it was great fun to perch on the backrest and stare in through the windows at us staring out at them. Then one day, not long after we had been letting them all out together, *Hermione* sat on the bench, stretched her neck....and gaped !

Disaster had struck again. We had made the fundamental mistake of not segregating new stock, and the Buffs had brought *mycoplasma* into our flock again. It was another visit to the vet, and again we had to inject them all morning and night. We were becoming very proficient at giving them their jabs, but couldn't afford the vet's bills. Luckily they all made a full recovery and we vowed never to make the same mistake again.

Our two bundles of fluff grew, and grew....and grew. We partitioned off a large section inside the shed on the allotment, and this became their home. Unfortunately the day came when one of them started crowing, closely followed by the other. How unlucky can you get? Six eggs bought, only two hatched – and both cockerels!

We fattened them up for a few months, and then the fateful day arrived when the first of them had to make the one-way trip to the oven. After my experiences trying to kill the sick birds I had been dreading having to do the deadly deed, and had been reading up on the subject at every opportunity and cross-examining everybody I met who kept chickens, trying to find the best way to do it.

I kept hearing about the 'broom handle method' and as this seemed to be a reliable, old fashioned way of quickly killing a chicken, I decided that it was the one for me. This method involves, would you believe it, a broom handle!

The idea is that you place the chicken on the ground and stretch its neck out, placing the broom handle across the neck. You then stand very lightly on either end of the handle to keep it in place, and hold onto the bird's legs. Switching your weight to the handle ends, you then pull back firmly and dislocate the neck.

That's the idea anyway, and everything went smoothly until the last part, when nothing much seemed to happen. I certainly never felt anything disjoint or snap, and so in desperation I heaved on the chooks ankles.

And fell flat on my backside!

There on the floor by the broom handle was a chickens head, and I was left holding onto the rest of the body, which was pumping blood from its severed neck, all down the front of my trousers. Shocked, I let go of its legs – and this was where I discovered an interesting new phenomenon. There is an old saying 'running around like a headless chicken' and I can assure you that it is true. They don't exactly run, but flap and flutter and thrash about, all the time pumping blood in all directions.

It was a horrific experience, but it did teach me a valuable lesson – that it is very difficult to tell when a chicken is dead! They don't come much deader than decapitated, and yet they still struggle and flap around. This is something that you have to come to terms with when raising chickens for the table, and in fact you have to start plucking them the instant that they are dead, to make the job easier. Plucking a bird that is still struggling and fighting can be very upsetting, so you need to know that it is definitely dead.

So, another bad experience to add to our growing list......but the chicken tasted wonderful and made a superb Sunday roast, accompanied by some of our first broad beans.

Yes, that's right, our first harvest had started to come in. We picked them very young and they were, as the old boy had promised, 'bootiful.'

We later found out that you can pick the whole pod when it is about three or four inches long, and slice it up and cook it like runner beans. This is a valuable early season food when your winter crops are nearly exhausted and spring crops not yet producing. In fact you can even pick the tips off the growing plants and eat them like spinach. Both these ideas came in very useful during our second spring when we hadn't yet learned the right amounts of each crop to plant and our food supplies ran very thin. The period between March and April was known many years ago as the 'Hungry Gap' and poor country folk often literally starved to death when spring crops didn't mature early enough. This is why so much of the autumn harvest was stored, dried, pickled, salted etc. – to provide food for the hungry gap.

However, I digress, but we harvested a really good quantity of broad beans, and froze lots for later use.

Another one of our early staple crops was peas, and these too cropped well. Podding them for freezing, we discovered that the organic farmer's lot isn't an easy one though, as we were sharing them with the progeny of the local population of pea moths! Nearly every pod was affected, and we were lucky if we managed to keep three peas from every five in each. Many people on the allotments spray their peas when they are in flower and this kills the maggots, but we have never been prepared to do this, preferring to share our crops if need be. We did find a way round it though – plant the peas under cloches in late autumn. They then crop a lot earlier the following year and have generally flowered before the dreaded pea moth emerges. As long as we pick the peas young we don't have a maggot problem.

We had discovered that growing your own food is a war between you and Mother Nature, and the second you turn your back on her she will attack you from a new direction. No matter how many battles or skirmishes you win, she always has a new weapon in her armoury.

However, we blithely pressed on, still not realising the huge tangled web that we were slowly being drawn into. We had very quickly realised that one plot wouldn't be enough to grow everything that we needed and within a couple of months we began to look at expanding. There were two plots to the rear of ours that didn't seem to have much activity going on, but we were told that they had been taken by a chap from London and his wife, who could only get down at the weekends but would soon be moving to Ipswich. As most of my gardening was carried out during the week, I never saw them.

The plot next to ours was pretty derelict, and we never saw anybody working on it, but in the autumn the huge crop of raspberries that it yielded attracted more than just the birds. A car pulled up one day and a man and woman got out and started picking the berries.

Chatting with them I discovered that the plot belonged to the chap's father, and he was now too old and frail to look after it and so they would probably be giving it up. As soon as they had left I galloped off to find the field secretary, and told him that I would like to take this one on too. He promised to let me know when he heard anything.

In fact, our plot was right at the edge of the civilised world, with nearly all the other allotments between ours and the perimeter fence heavily overgrown with eight foot high brambles. For some reason our corner of the field had been pretty much abandoned, whilst the rest of them (and there were a lot) were nicely cultivated. There are nearly two hundred separate plots on our fields, with a similarly sized allotment half a mile or so down the road, so our area is fairly well provided for.

The overgrown fields meant that my plot was a peaceful retreat though, and there was plentiful wildlife, especially birds. Jays, green woodpeckers, sparrowhawks and long tailed tits were just some of the more unusual residents. Muntjac deer were sometimes seen emerging from the bramble thickets, but the curious thing was that we never saw any evidence of rabbits.

Rabbits can be a serious pest if you are trying to raise greenstuff, and in view of the huge amount of food available, their absence was a mystery...until we noticed all the footprints that appeared every night in newly dug and raked soil. Nice big dog fox prints and smaller vixen pawmarks. They were obviously keeping the rabbit population under control. I was so glad that I had made my chook run very fox-proof.

I often worked until it was too dark to see to do any more, and about half an hour before sunset the foxes would emerge and begin to prowl around the fields looking for prey. Later, when they had young in their earth, they were often seen in broad daylight, searching for food for the hungry youngsters.

The two plots at the rear of ours saw a little activity. A large home-made shed appeared backing onto our chicken run, and all the weeds covering both plots suddenly turned brown and shrivelled a few days later. The Londoners had obviously visited, armed with a big bottle of weed killer. A big steaming heap of horse muck materialised shortly afterwards – clearly things were progressing and we expected digging operations to begin. Nothing happened though and the weeds began to grow again.

I worked away at clearing my plot and getting it dug over and raked ready for cultivation, enjoying the peace and quiet and the outdoor life. I was busy digging one morning when a stranger appeared and headed for the derelict plot next to mine. I was somewhat surprised when he started clearing away the undergrowth, and when I asked him what he was up to he introduced himself as the new plot owner. I was gobsmacked and promptly stomped off to find the field secretary.

When I angrily tackled him about my new neighbour he calmly told me that he had forgotten that I wanted it. I was furious!

The only plots available were of the jungle variety, and I really didn't fancy tackling them, but my ears pricked up when the field secretary said that he had heard a rumour that the people from London had moved to Ipswich and then the chap had died. He had no telephone number for them, but gave me their address.

Feeling a little ghoulish, Sue and I set off to visit his widow.

Any Fool Can Be A.......

It transpired that the rumours were true and her husband (who had spent months looking forward to his retirement and his allotments) had tragically died suddenly almost as soon as they moved house. She couldn't manage the allotments as well as the huge garden in her new home, and so she was happy for us to take them over.

We inherited two plots densely covered in a mixture of live and dead weeds, a shed and a huge heap of horse muck. We were still using it until quite recently, when goat muck took over – but that's another story for later.

Sue puts her foot down

…and stands in something unpleasant for the umpteenth time.

O ur garden chooks had learned that mummy sometimes brought something nice for them when she appeared, and so the back doorstep had become their gathering place. Unfortunately they all felt so grateful for her presents that they felt obliged to leave her gifts of their own, of the brown, squishy variety!

One day she put her foot down and squished once too often, so she put her foot down firmly – the chooks had to go.

It had been nice having them free range in the garden in some ways – they were always up to something interesting so you could watch them for hours – but on the other hand they totally devastated our lovely landscaped and well-planted flower beds. What they didn't eat got scratched up when they created dust baths everywhere. We didn't have a problem with lily beetle any more as the chooks ate all the grubs, but on the other hand we didn't have any lilies either!

We now had plenty of room on the allotments with the two extra plots, so we decided to expand the chicken runs over there, and in future we would only keep chicks and youngsters at home.

'Chicks and youngsters?' I hear you querying. Yes, we had gone into hatching in a big way. We had started with a borrowed incubator that held 10 eggs, but were quickly hooked and bought our own 24-egg model with an automatic turning cradle. That may all sound a bit complicated, but really it isn't. A mother hen will regularly turn all the eggs under her with her beak so that the membrane inside doesn't dry out and the chick die, and when artificially hatching we have to mimic this. With the cheaper incubators you have to do this laboriously by hand, turning each individual egg three or four times a day, which is pretty difficult if you are at work all day. Our borrowed model was a step up from this as it was octagonal shaped, and you simply turned the whole machine to one side and then the other. You still had to be there to do it, but it was much less fiddly.

Our new whizzy incubator sat in a cradle that gently rocked it backwards and forwards 24 hours a day, and the hatch results were excellent. Initially we had kept chicks on the sideboard in the living room in brooders made from large plastic storage boxes, with an anglepoise lamp over them to keep them warm, but we soon found that they produce *loads* of dust and so they were moved to the spare bedroom. We found an indoor rabbit cage cheaply at a local auction, and as the chicks grew they were moved into this. I'm not sure whether the dust is created by the chicks themselves as they shed their baby fluff and grow feathers, or whether it comes from their chick crumb food, but the amount of it became totally unacceptable. Now that we were producing larger numbers of chicks, every surface of the room and its contents became coated in a thick layer of dust very quickly.

Any Fool Can Be A.......

Our solution was to build a long box with a wired lid, which fitted nicely under the window in our garden shed, and we suspended a heat lamp over it. These lamps are intended for keeping young orphaned lambs etc. warm, but are ideal for poultry. The box sides protected the young chicks from draughts, and they had plenty of room as the box is five feet long and two feet wide. We still had dust and lots of it, but at least it wasn't indoors. The eerie red glow from the lamp must have worried the neighbours at night though as the shed looked to be on fire!

We eventually discovered dull emitter bulbs, which give out heat but no light.

So now we had lots of lovely space on the allotments the chooks naturally had to expand to fill the available space, didn't they?

I managed to get hold of some building site security fencing. You know the stuff – six feet high steel wire fencing, in sections eleven feet long. It is absolutely perfect for making chook runs and slightly damaged panels can be picked up quite cheaply from hire companies.

Notice that word 'cheaply' as it will begin to feature more and more in this story. We were sinking into the downshifting mire without noticing, and gradually adjusting to living on a smaller and smaller income.

Six of these panels made a superb chicken run. We still had no housing, and couldn't afford to buy an expensive new house, but the solution was soon found.

We had splashed out on Ebay and bought a cheap trailer – there's that word 'cheap' again. Note the other word 'Ebay' which has already appeared once or twice as 'cheap' and 'Ebay' will combine more and more as our tale progresses.

In case you are the one person on the planet who has never heard of Ebay, it is an Internet auction site where you can buy anything from anybody anywhere in the world. If you don't know what the Internet is, then I think that you should put this book down and go and sit quietly in a darkened room.

Finally (for now) I will introduce you to another word – 'Freeads' or local newspapers. People can advertise in them free, but you have to buy the paper. Unless of course you read the classified adverts for free online. Actually, that's another word I like – 'free.' On reflection it is my favourite word!

We decided that we would get a secondhand shed and convert it, rather than buy a chook house ready made, and we found one cheaply(!) in the Freeads in Norfolk. Our new trailer was about five feet long by three and a half wide with low side walls. Our new shed purchase was six feet long by four feet wide, so the whole thing had to be strapped perilously to the top of the trailer. We managed to get it the forty miles home safely though, without mishap or interference from the local Old Bill, and it was erected inside our new steel run. It was beginning to look more like a POW camp every day!

The shed was big enough to comfortably house the ten week old youngsters we had at home, so they were brought straight over and settled in.

I came over to feed them the next morning to find a window broken and the chooks huddled in a corner with their feeder lying beside them. Hooligans had visited the allotments overnight, breaking into around fifty sheds. They had cut the padlock off my shed and were probably frustrated to find chickens not tools, so they smashed the window and threw the feeder at the youngsters. Luckily the strong wind had blown the door shut or we would have lost the chickens to the foxes for sure. It was a bitterly cold snowy January night, and I still wonder now why these kids didn't have something better to do.....

We finished off the run by sinking chainlink fencing into the ground all the way round to stop old foxy digging his way in, and fixing fishing netting across the top.

An old boy on the allotments had bought a huge roll (cheaply!) at auction and then decided he didn't want it, so I bought it from him. I found a million uses for it, and I will bore you with all of them later. The shed was fitted with perches, a pophole cut in the door, and some nestboxes fitted to the outside. We were in business!

I quickly realised that the run was very big for our number of birds, and so I partitioned one corner off using some aviary panels bought through the local classifieds, and installed a small roosting house found through the same source.

By now I was in chook overdrive and built across between the two runs creating two more pens, and we were travelling all over East Anglia picking up birds. Hatching eggs were arriving from all over the country, and the incubator was going flat out. The situation was becoming unsustainable unless we were prepared to build over all our plots.

The trouble was I had fallen in love with the Sussex breed, and it came in so many different colours and I wanted them all! Then of course there were bantams as well as large fowl. Then Wyandottes caught my eye with their beautiful colours......and I was offered some Buff Orpington eggs.

Eventually I ground to a halt and realised that I had become obsessed with chickens, something that should only be a small part of what we were trying to do. But what *were* we trying to do?

What had started as a desire for a bit of fresh veg and a few eggs was developing into something life changing.

Even the arrival of avian influenza, or bird flu, on our shores didn't put us off keeping chickens. Whilst the media whipped everybody into a frenzy and insisted that we were all going to die horrible deaths, and the government began registering poultry keepers as though we were all convicted criminals, we doggedly carried on with our plans. We were informed that if an outbreak occurred nearby we would have to put all our birds under cover so that they couldn't come into contact with wild bird droppings. This wasn't practical for us with our long range of interlinked runs, so we bought a couple of huge tarpaulins and loads of finely meshed plastic netting. The idea was that if our allotments were suddenly declared to be in a protection zone due to an outbreak nearby, we would cover the runs with the tarpaulin and wrap the side walls with the birdproof netting. We waited nervously for a few weeks, then bunged the whole lot up in the loft.

By the autumn of our first full growing season we had had plenty of highs and lows. One of the highs was a superb crop of the most amazingly tasty strawberries. Their incredible scent drove our taste buds mad, and it was as much as we could do to pick them and carry them home without scoffing the lot on the way. Broad beans picked young were a sensation, and runner beans and peas cooked straight from the plants tasted so much better than shop bought.

Sweetcorn proved to be a revelation! I was wandering around the allotments one morning when I spotted somebody sitting in his shed munching away on a raw sweetcorn cob. My 'Yuk' comment resulted in my being told that I didn't know what I was missing, or words to that effect that I can't repeat here, so I headed back to my own patch and immediately tried one. Of course I then had to gallop home and take one to Sue for her to try. She was equally dubious to start with, and equally amazed by the wonderful taste.

Sweetcorn cobs have to be picked at exactly the right moment to get them in their prime. Too early and they aren't ripe, too late and they are mealy or floury. Picked and eaten raw at the right moment, they are as juicy as an apple. They may be too sweet for some people's tastes, but I have a sweet tooth and love them. There is an old saying that you should be boiling the saucepan of water ready before you pick sweetcorn, so that you can cook them instantly as the sugar begins to turn to starch as soon as they are picked. It's definitely true – so how can you ever *hope* to eat shop-bought sweetcorn at their best?

I told you about the peas, but did I mention the peapod wine? When you are on the slippery slope to going M.A.D. nothing gets wasted, and once we had podded and frozen the peas themselves, their pods were used to produce an excellent (and very strong!) wine.

Remember those overgrown plots of brambles I mentioned? Well they yielded twenty pounds or so of wonderful blackberries which magically became five gallons of potent red wine. We had rescued some blackcurrant bushes that another gardener was digging up and dumping the previous autumn, and they produced a good yield. Neither of us like blackcurrants so they became, you guessed it, an excellent vintage blackcurrant wine.

We also acquired some gooseberry bushes from a derelict plot and these produced a really heavy crop. The berries were rather sharp. On reflection, and with the benefit of hindsight, we probably picked them too early – but what the hell, it was an excuse for another couple of gallons of excellent wine.

So by now we were becoming alcoholic chook-keepers!

Our potato crop was slightly affected by blight, but we still had a good yield, and the extra protein in the form of maggots in the peas did us no harm. Our son discovered a cooked caterpillar in his cabbage one Sunday and was told to be quiet or everybody would want one. Home grown fruit and veg aren't the boring uniform shape that you buy in the supermarket, neither are they blemish-free or free from trespassers. Supermarket tomatoes don't have funny faces with noses, their carrots don't have two legs and a willie and their potatoes don't have interesting craters in them where the slugs have been excavated. In fact, supermarket food is dead boring really!

Autumn-planted Japanese onions were excellent – so juicy that they spat and sizzled deliciously when cooked and made you weep bucketfuls whilst peeling them. We tasted marrow for the first time ever, and also (following the urgings of a neighbour) Spaghetti Squash. This unusual and exotic vegetable has a distinctive and different taste and texture, and we are pretty sure that something in it is a diuretic as we both find that we need to make lots of 'visits' after eating it.

Carrots, on the other hand, were a disaster – small and woody due to being planted in a patch of dead soil. Although about two thirds of the plot had been recently manured and was very fertile, the remainder had had nothing for years as the soil had no goodness in it whatsoever. A second sowing of carrots in good soil were totally destroyed by carrotfly. Carrotfly became the bane of our lives over the next couple of years. We obviously had a superhuman variety breeding on our allotments, as even a two foot high barrier around later carrots failed to keep them out. They are supposedly unable to get over anything higher than eighteen inches, so I'm entering some of ours in the pole vault at the next Olympics. It's the only explanation I can come up with for their devastating success.

Something maggoty also destroyed our turnips and swedes, so root crops were a failure all round really.

The blackbirds stole a lot of our redcurrants. They made a damn good try at the strawberries too, until I made some covers for the beds from rigid plastic netting – bought cheaply at auction. We didn't know it, but the blackbirds were a portent of things to come. Not only was the local flora determined to give us a hard time in the shape of *Fat Hen* and *Gallant Soldier,* but the resident fauna was going to join in. Oh boy was it going to join in!

Free and cycling

Fuel prices were now rising alarmingly, and lorry drivers took to the roads in big convoys to block the motorways and waste more expensive diesel, not to mention petrol in the hundreds of cars stuck behind them in the queues that formed as they exercised their democratic right to protest. They were escorted by police cars, which prevented the rest of us from exercising our democratic right to thump the lorry drivers.

We were using our car less and less now as we couldn't afford to do much anyway, but the petrol prices made it even more difficult for us. Sue decided to get herself a bike so that she could nip down to the town without paying bus fares, which had also risen steeply, and I decided to get one too so that I could cycle to work. Cycling would get us fit and healthy and be good for us.

Nothing to do with downshifting of course, we're not going M.A.D.

We started saving up, searching the local paper for bargains and checking the offerings at the cycle auction to see what we could find, but then my mother said she would buy us new ones – aren't mothers wonderful? We bought big double pannier bags for the bikes and backpacks for ourselves too.

The weekly supermarket run was now done on bikes, and if we couldn't fit it in the panniers and backpacks we didn't buy it, so that kept the shopping bill down.....although we sometimes strapped bigger things on top of the panniers with bungee rubbers. By the end of our first growing season we were already down to buying only essential basics such as washing and cleaning materials, cereals, sugar, milk – items that we couldn't produce or make ourselves.

I could even bring home a twenty kilo sack of chicken feed on my bike!

M.A.D. ? ...Definitely not.

To be honest, cycling really *is* good for you, and we both lost weight. It also makes you feel younger because you can go back to your youth and break the law by cycling on the pavement and ride around with no lights on at night.

I managed to con my employers...:...sorry......*persuade* my employers that I needed one of those dayglow luminous safety coats for my work, and it is great as a cycle jacket. I think they work by dazzling motorists so that they swerve and knock down pedestrians instead of cyclists.

Having reawakened the pleasure of cycling we now combined it with our favourite word – 'free.'

We discovered the world of Freecycle.

Any Fool Can Be A.......

Never heard of it? Well to a downshifter (not that we were downshifters!) it is the best thing since sliced bread. It is an organisation that helps you get rid of stuff you don't want any more.

It works via an email mailing list. You simply post an advert to the list telling them what you are giving away and then take cover as the screaming hordes head your way. No, not really, as interested parties have to email you back to get your details, but if you want something you have to act FAST!

We found that being at home during the day was a great advantage as you have a head start over people that are at work.

We found that it is generally the slightly better-off who are giving stuff away; people who can't be bothered to sell it through classifieds or at car boot sales, and some of them get a buzz from giving to 'charity cases' and speak to you a little condescendingly, but hey, who cares - it's free!

Our best find was an almost brand new bread maker which has been getting used two or three times a week for the last three years or so, but we also replaced our broken down stereo via Freecycle, and got quite a few other freebies too. They eventually brought in a rationing system where they kept track of who was claiming what as they suspected that somebody was grabbing everything and selling it at car boot sales. We quietly left the group.

Having reminded myself about Freecycle now I really should rejoin it, but perhaps under a new name in case they still remember me.

The eagle-eyed amongst you will have noticed that I have slipped another new word past you, or rather three new words – 'car,' 'boot' and 'sale.'

I have heard so many people say that car boot sales are a waste of time as they are just full of rubbish. A polite enquiry as to what time they visited them generally gets the answer, "Oh, nine or ten o'clock." Well, of course they were full of rubbish – THEY WERE TOO LATE GETTING THERE!!

Dedicated 'Bootees' are out and about at five or six o'clock, when the tables are covered in dew and you need a torch to examine the goodies on offer. You also need padded elbows so that you can jab the dealers out of the way, a thick skin so that you can make outrageously low offers for any treasures that you find and ear muffs so that you can't hear the vendor's rude refusals. As you get more experienced you will recognise the more rapacious dealers by the shape of their backsides, because you will see them sticking out of the boots of cars every week as they virtually climb in and help promising-looking sellers to unpack.

By seven o'clock there is an army of ants making their way back to their own cars, struggling under huge loads of plundered bargains.

We have found countless excellent buys at car boots, and most Sundays and bank holidays we can be found trekking round our favourite sales. As I type this I have just found myself a brand new pair of very expensive steel toe-capped work boots for eight quid. A rare find for somebody who needs size 13s.

We have also made the occasional bad purchase too as there is no way of checking that electrical things actually work, and sometimes we have arrived home only to find an essential part broken or missing. It's a chance you take, but by and large we are winning the game.

But just when everything seemed to be going swimmingly, disaster struck, and it was due to one of those *bad* boot sale buys.

Any Fool Can Be A.......

I had just started back at the winter seed company job, having been recalled for my second season. The first season part-timers get laid off first when the work dies away, so I was in a more secure position, and enjoyed the work.

The pathways on the allotments were a pain to keep neat and tidy, so when I spotted a petrol strimmer at a boot sale I snapped it up. It proved to be very useful but was a bit of a pain to get started sometimes, needing a lot of pulling on the starter rope. One day it was in a particularly perverse mood and I tugged and tugged to no avail, until I finally threw it back into the shed in disgust.

The next morning I woke up, turned over.....and screamed! My right arm was in absolute agony. It turned out that I had torn a tendon in my elbow, the condition known as 'tennis elbow,' and my arm was totally useless.

I phoned in sick to the seed company, put my arm in a sling, took copious quantities of anti-inflammatory pills and painkillers and sat around moping.

Only rest would heal it, I was told by the doctor, so rest I did. By the end of the week the joint was a little more mobile, and when I got a phone call from the seed company asking how I was getting on I said that I thought I would be back at work the following week. I was flabbergasted when I was told not to bother as there were no orders coming in, so I was laid off. No, not flabbergasted – furious!

No amount of arguing would make the manager change her mind – I was out on my ear. What a heartless bunch.

The supermarket by comparison were brilliant. Despite being known as a ruthless company, they looked after me well. I was placed on light duties which, as I was working in the produce department (ironic, eh?), were still fairly hard work.

The allotments were a different story - I was unable to do much at all. When you are self-employed just about the worst thing you can do is injure yourself, and my damaged elbow meant that I could do very little. Luckily it happened in September and so I had the winter to get over it, which was just as well as I was warned it would be a long job.

A long job it certainly was. Even the light duties at the supermarket involved lifting, and the elbow wouldn't heal. A week of rest would see an improvement, and then I would go into work for one day and be back to square one. After six months I was still in agony and now couldn't do the essential work on the allotments. Sue had to help me get the seed potatoes planted as I couldn't dig at all.

We clearly couldn't carry on like this as we were in financial difficulties now as well, having lost my normal winter income at the seed company.

I needed an office job and it had to be for more than one day a week, but there was nothing on the vacancies board at the supermarket. Eventually I had to reluctantly tell my manager that I was handing in my notice as I just couldn't do the job any more.

He refused to accept it and said that he would have a word with the personnel manager. Within twenty four hours I was offered an office job for three days a week. Once again my guardian angel had stepped in and looked after me.

The elbow still took a further six months to heal, and that was only after a risky cortisone injection into the damaged tendon, where I faced the danger of snapping the tendon altogether. It wasn't healing though, so I had to take that chance, and luckily it all went well.

I tried to take more care of myself after this frustrating episode but history was destined to repeat itself, only in a much sillier way this time.

In the meantime we decided that we needed more fruit production. The superb strawberries had whetted our appetite for other juicy delicacies.

One of the new plots had been used for potatoes in the first year.

A big mistake. Well not really a mistake; spuds are a good way to break in new ground – more a case of ignorance and inexperience spoiling things.

Although heavily weedkillered, the plot was a mass of speargrass which appeared to be dead but wasn't. We found this out after we had planted the potatoes, when grass sprang up again everywhere. Do you know just how tough the 'spears' are on speargrass? They grew straight through our potato crop, but that wasn't the worst of it. If we had raised our maincrop spuds early there wouldn't have been a problem, but my damaged arm made lifting them difficult and we were late digging them up......

The crop was riddled with wireworm.

We found out afterwards that the adults lay their eggs in grass, and, had we lifted the crop one month earlier, we would have saved it. Worse still, the damn things can take three years to clear from a piece of ground.

So, no more spuds in that plot. We decided to use part of it for an orchard, and as one of our neighbours had a discovery apple that produced a huge harvest of tasty fruit, we plumped for one of those. Despite having no money we realised that cheap trees are a false economy, as apart from anything else you only get a twig if you buy a one year old plant and have a long wait to get any fruit. We made a trip out to Ken Muir's establishment and duly bought a three year old pot grown minaret. A minaret is a space-saving tree that has its side spur branches kept short and its overall height limited, the idea being that you can keep more trees in a smaller space and still get a heavy crop.

Thus our orchard was born – maybe not from the proverbial single acorn, but perhaps from the seed of an idea. I had a bit of birthday money and so could afford a second tree, but didn't have a clue what type to go for. We had spotted an advert for an 'Apple Tasting Day' at Ken Muir's, and so off we trotted to the wilds of Weeley again for a look-see. It turned out to be a very worthwhile trip as we could taste something like 200 apples and pears to see which ones suited our palettes. The great man himself sat on his throne cheerfully answering questions from a long queue of budding or bewildered fruit growers. He was no spring chicken so he did well to last the day really. For those of you that don't know; Ken was the fruit expert on BBC TV's 'Gardener's World' for many years.

The results of the apple tasting came as a great surprise to both of us. Neither of us ever fancied russet apples, as we found the brown woody-looking skins unappealing, so to discover their amazing taste was a revelation. Mr. Muir duly relieved us of another twenty five notes and we trundled home with a Herefordshire Russet taking over the back of the car.

We broke our own rules by buying a couple more apple trees – a Worcester Pearmain and a Cox's Orange Pippin – cheaply from a market stall, and they have never really done very well. The Cox's produced fruit in its second year but hasn't done very well since, and the Pearmain fruits have blotchy skins. This tree had one branch die, which I removed and burned, but I suspect that there is a canker or something similar present. I think it will soon have a new home on the bonfire. There's a lot to be said for guaranteed virus-free stock, if you can afford them.

Our infant orchard looked very sparse, but it was a start.

When I was on the allotments one autumn morning I spotted a strange little tractor trundling in towing a big cage trailer crammed full of leaves. The driver manoeuvred around a bit, backed onto somebody's plot, and then the trailer lifted and tipped the whole load into a big bin built from corrugated iron. The tractor drove off and left the allotments, and left me intrigued! An hour or so later it was back with another load and tipped it on a different plot. I had noticed huge leaf mould containers on several plots and wondered how the owners had managed to sweep up so many leaves – I was beginning to understand now.

On enquiring I discovered that this was a local council tractor which was fitted with a huge vacuum cleaner thingy underneath which sucked up leaves and blew them into the towed trailer. The driver patrolled the huge park across the road from the allotments, clearing up the fallen leaves, and then had the job of disposing of them. He was only too happy to bring them to people on our fields who wanted them.

Now leaf mould is *wonderful* stuff if rotted down for a year or two and then dug into the soil. It adds a lot of nutrients, but more importantly it is a huge help with moisture retention. The soil on our allotments is very light indeed, in fact if you dig down a little way you hit pure sand, and in dry spells the plots turn into little more than dust bowls. Fifty or sixty years of being allotments, with gardeners digging in huge quantities of manure and anything organic, has helped considerably, but the depth of topsoil varies a lot from plot to plot.

I needed some of these leaves…..no, I needed a *lot* of these leaves, and I needed them fast – most of the trees had already dropped them, so the supply wouldn't last long. I quickly built a big pen on the end of the orchard plot which backed onto the roadway. Luckily I still had a lot of the heavy rigid plastic netting which was ideal, and I used it to construct a cage the whole width of the plot, about ten feet deep and three feet high. I didn't realise quite how many leaves a cage this big would hold – it seems the trailer holds around two tons at a time, and the chap made about ten trips to fill it! That's one hell of a lot of leaves!

They had to be raked to the back of the cage after each load was tipped to make room for the next load, and it was hard work, but it was worth it in the end.

My motives for wanting these leaves were actually twofold. Yes, I wanted to rot them down and dig them into my plots, but I also wanted to use them as a deep litter in my chicken runs. These had a tendency to turn into gooey swamps after heavy rain.

The chooks were intrigued when I started wheelbarrowing in loads of leaves, and this curiosity turned to delight when I filled their runs six inches deep with them.

They spend hours scratching away in the litter searching for tasty titbits, constantly turning it over. This keeps it fresh and it gradually breaks down and sinks into the soil. Combined with their droppings, old green stuff and other food it produces wonderful, rich compost. I dig the runs out each autumn and spread the superb stuff on my veg plots.

It gets windy

With the two extra plots we had lots of ground spare, and so we looked around for something to fill up a bit of one of them. I had noticed some very tall plants growing on a few plots, and enquiries revealed that these were Jerusalem artichokes. I had never heard of them, although I knew of the traditional artichoke which is a huge thistle, and you eat the flower bud. It is considered a delicacy.

Jerusalems were apparently very easy to grow and were more like potatoes.

They sounded like a good candidate for our spare ground and so I duly ordered a box of organically grown seed artichoke tubers from an Internet site, and waited for them to arrive at planting time. They arrived a bit early and there was still snow on the ground, so I had to keep them for a couple of weeks. If you can get a fork in the ground then conditions are fine for artichoke tubers to be planted, so a couple of weeks later they went in. I planted them beside the chook run as I figured these tall plants would be good wind breaks, and there were so many of them that I had two rows across the full width of the plot.

Imagine my surprise when a month later another boxful turned up.

Another two rows were planted out beside the earlier ones.

It turned out that they really *are* very easy to grow – in fact, just try stopping them! They also grow very fast, and every single tuber grew. We had four rows of seven feet high plants, and the only care they needed was to turn the hose on them if conditions got really dry and to cut the flower heads off as they crop better if not allowed to flower. We eagerly awaited the bumper crop, and in due course it was ready and we dug up the first tubers.

Sue decided to boil them, and we tried them as a potato substitute with a roast dinner. They had a delicate flavour that we both enjoyed, and we were well pleased with the decision to try them. About half an hour after our meal the room erupted in a cacophony of sound.

With a violent eruption of 'tooting' and 'parping' we suddenly discovered that Jerusalem artichokes give you terrible wind!

They were immediately christened 'fartychokes,' and that's what we have called them ever since. We tried cooking them in various ways, including making a delicious soup from them, but they always had the same devastating effect.

Sue eventually banned them from the kitchen and I didn't even bother digging the rest up.

Now fartychokes are remarkably tenacious, and every single one of the crop of tubers sprouted again the following season. Instead of four rows we had an absolute jungle thicket of them in the second year. I didn't need the piece of ground that they were in, and ignored them, but they multiplied each year......although eventually I found a use for them.

You'll have to wait a bit to hear about that though.

In the meantime, we had expanded still further. You will recall that the field secretary gave the plot next to us to a newcomer? The young chap was very keen. He got an old shed from somewhere, and he painstakingly rebuilt a secondhand greenhouse on his plot. He dug the whole piece of ground over, established an asparagus bed and planted crops of all sorts. He talked a very good allotment. In fact he would talk to anybody that would listen – and for longer than they were interested in listening. In fact, if there was an Olympic event for talking about allotments he would undoubtedly have won the gold medal. He talked endlessly to me about my chickens, and announced his intention of taking on the jungle plot next to him to use for raising them. He talked too about his plans for new crops and he talked about football. In fact he talked about…well, anything really.

I would spot him chatting to somebody at the other end of the field, then to somebody else, then somebody else. You get the picture, don't you?

He would talk with authority about the soil pH and all things technical, and I would just nod knowingly.

One day he asked me if I preferred a trowel or a hand fork for weeding. "Neither, I prefer to hand weed," I replied.

"So what gloves do you use, cotton or rubber?"

"Neither, I use my hands."

"What about stinging nettles?"

"What about them?"

"What do you use to weed them?"

"My hands."

"Don't you get stung?"

"Yes, but after a day or two of getting stung they don't hurt you any more."

He stared at me with a mixture of shock, disbelief and incomprehension.

The problem was that whilst he was busy talking to all and sundry, the weeds were sneaking back. He made desultory attempts at hoeing, but the weeds clearly demoralised him.

His visits to the plot became more infrequent, and it became overgrown and then one morning I arrived to find some women digging up potatoes from in amongst the weeds on his plot. When I asked what was going on, I was told that matey had suddenly just quit and handed his keys in, and they had enquired about a second plot and the secretary had given it to them. I was furious for a second time, although in fairness I hadn't told the secretary that I was still interested.

The next morning when I got there they were all huddled around their shed. It had been broken into during the night.

The next morning they were dismantling the greenhouse. They had decided to give up this patch as the plot next to their original one had become vacant and so they were taking that one. They were liberating the greenhouse and anything moveable/harvestable before departing.

A quick phone call to the secretary and we had secured our fourth allotment.

We now had a quarter of an acre of land and on the new plot were two rows of autumn raspberries that we inherited. They cropped a couple of weeks after we took the field on, and we harvested THIRTY FIVE POUNDS of superb, tasty raspberries over the next four weeks or so.

So, why four plots when we hadn't filled the other three yet? Well,

Any Fool Can Be A.......

I had a cunning plan. I wanted a polytunnel. Were we going M.A.D. ? Maybe just a little bit.

We were gradually getting more into the whole ethos of being green/saving food miles and self-sufficiency, and wanted a polytunnel for various reasons really.

We were freezing a lot of our produce to use during the winter, but wanted to try to eat more seasonally. I was always getting up on my soapbox whenever anybody would listen, ranting about the way that we as a nation have stopped eating seasonally. When I was a boy I really looked forward to June because it meant we had strawberries for dessert. They only lasted a few short weeks then they were over and we moved onto something else as the harvest came in. If we wanted anything out of season it was tinned peaches or pears. Now strawberries are in the supermarkets all the year round. They are grown in Israel or Spain or Outer Mongolia or somewhere else equally far away and are flown to the UK.

Most of them are grown hydroponically – this means grown in troughs of water with nutrients added – and they have no taste whatsoever. The whole thing makes me despair. Virtually every item of fruit or vegetable that we eat is now available just about 365 days a year, but at what cost to the planet?

The idea was that the tunnel would extend our growing season – getting veg started much earlier in the year, and protecting them into late autumn. We also wanted to grow crops that needed better weather or a longer growing season than our English climate can provide.

Well that was the plan, but due to our very restricted finances it was going to prove a difficult one to complete. Our only hope was to find a secondhand frame, and we discovered that they are *very* sought after. The few that appeared in local papers were snapped up instantly or too much money, and on Ebay they made enormous prices even when in poor condition. It proved to be a very long search.

Our poultry explosion continued, with us travelling all over the east of England (and sometimes much further) to acquire new stock.

At this time there were regular weekly poultry auctions at several livestock markets in towns and villages around us, and one of our favourites was held every Saturday morning in Colchester. We were there one weekend when a lot came up that was most interesting – a Light Sussex bantam hen and her brood of six chicks. We got them for a reasonable price and the chicks turned out to be three boys and three girls. The girls turned out to be exceptionally good broodies, and became foster mums to many chicks. The original mum didn't live very long though, perhaps a year. We later found out that this is a good way of disposing of older hens – sell them with a batch of young chicks as a job lot and get a good price for an old, otherwise unsaleable bird.

A couple of months later we were back at the same auction. We had been trying to find some more large fowl Buff Sussex for a while, and one week there at the auction was a box containing six pretty young buffs, about 6 weeks old. Another box contained a couple of buffs and a couple of lights, all of similar ages. We were so pleased to see them, and speculated on how much they would go for. The mixed box came up first and we were surprised that it reached quite a high price, around £25 I seem to remember. We couldn't afford to pay more than about twenty quid for our lot, so we were rather resigned to the fact that we wouldn't get them.

The auctioneer started the bids at a fiver for six chicks 'as hatched,' meaning that this was the complete brood, but there were no takers. Sue and I looked at one another, I winked and we waited.

Any Fool Can Be A.......

After a pause he dropped the bidding to a couple of pounds, and my hand shot up. He took a couple of other bids against me and I was now paying a fiver. The bidding stopped. We had won six Buff Sussex youngsters for a measly five pounds! It was only some time later, when I became much more experienced at auctions, that I realised that the reserve price was five pounds, and he had taken bids 'off the wall' or imaginary bids, to run me up to the minimum selling price. This is a common practice at auctions and it was only when we saw furniture that had previously supposedly been sold reappearing at later sales that we twigged what was going on. In this instance it didn't matter, because we had got the chooks for a price that we considered to be a bargain.

We decided that we would eat any cocks and raise the hens up to the egg-laying stage, when they would be added into our Buff Sussex breeding flock. This would vary the gene pool a bit and perhaps help to improve our birds. Our existing Buffs were in fact almost the colour of Red Sussex, so getting some lighter coloured birds into the mix would perhaps tone the colour down a little.

The chicks grew rapidly. They looked a bit leggy, and were a little slow in feathering up fully, but I put this down to them perhaps having been taken away from their mother a little early. Then they all suddenly really bolted upwards and became very lanky and skinny.......and eventually one of them crowed. They all started squaring up to one another and puffing out their neck hackles. Before long it was like a cock-fighting ring, with all six of them fighting.

We had bought six young cockerels!

The brood wasn't as hatched at all, but the boys had been very carefully separated from the girls. We had been palmed off with the unwanted boys.

Eventually we were to learn that with experience you could begin to sex your hatchlings from just a few days old, judging them by their stance, leg thickness and certain details of their feather growth and development. It is not easy to do, but with a practised eye you can figure out in your mind that you have perhaps seven girls and five boys in a hatch of twelve and rarely be wrong.

Whoever had entered these birds into the auction had almost certainly been accomplished at sexing them from an early age, and had kept his young pullets and got rid of the boys. Very clever.

To be fair, it may not have been that as we once hatched out a brood of seven Red Sussex and the whole lot turned out to be cocks, but because it was an auction I'm convinced that we were conned. None of the experienced auction attendees bid against us, so I'm sure that they knew that the seller did this regularly.

Perhaps they were even tipped off.

Who knows? We put it down to experience, had six cheap roast dinners, and moved on.

I think it was about this time that we realised that local small auctions were used as a dumping ground for unwanted chooks, and we stopped going. The big famous specialist auctions were another matter altogether......

We reached the stage of having over 100 birds on the allotment and at home, and I realised that my passion for breeding all the colours of (mainly) Sussex chickens had gotten a bit out of control. I had lost sight of the reason for keeping chickens in the first place – originally a few eggs and later for meat. We didn't need this many chickens and they were eating us out of house and home. They also took a considerable amount of looking after, especially when there were chicks to take care of.

Any Fool Can Be A.......

As we are not big meat eaters we decided to concentrate on bantams, and so we sold most of the large fowl, including our lovely Red Sussex. This is an extremely rare colour and we had some magnificent birds. Selling them was something I regretted later. We had managed to find large fowl breeding groups of all colours except the extremely rare Coronation Sussex. This variety is like a Light Sussex except that all the black areas are replaced by a dove grey. This gives the bird a softer look, very pretty. Only a few people have them, and they are very difficult to obtain. Large fowl Brown Sussex and Silver Sussex are probably rarer, to be honest, but are not as sought after.

So we specialised in Light and Buff Sussex bantams as they eat so much less than large fowl. By mating a cock Light Sussex to a hen Buff Sussex we could sex the offspring with 100% accuracy. The orangey coloured chicks were female, and the yellow ones male. The females were purebred Buff Sussex whilst the males were Lights, but carried the gold gene and would show a yellow tinge to their white plumage as they grew. The girls could be safely sold or traded at any age and the boys would make a one-way visit to the oven. Actually no, that sounds like Sue's cooking is so bad that they got incinerated!

We even managed to find some Coronation Sussex bantams. Admittedly they aren't as rare as the large fowl, but they are still hard to obtain. I spotted some for sale in the catalogue of the Salisbury poultry auctions and was lucky enough to know somebody going there, who bid for and won a cock Coronation Sussex and two Splash hens. We galloped down to the New Forest the next day to collect them from him.

You're not a chicken keeper, are you? You're wondering what a 'splash' is. Okay, well without boring you to death, the Coronation colouring does not breed true – if you mate two of them together you will get percentages of Coronations, Lights and Splashes.

A Splash is basically a white bird with (usually) tiny patches of the grey colouring here and there. A splash cock is no good for breeding (unless you are desperate) as you can't judge the quality of his colouring well enough to assess potential. The Coronation colouring is not that strong and a Light has to be re-introduced into the breeding mix every couple of years to maintain quality. The pairing that we bought would produce a mixture of offspring. The ideal pairing is a Light Sussex cock with Splash hens, as this will yield 100% Coronation chicks.

Just to really confuse you, all of this refers only to the British Coronation and involves the blue gene. The Australians (who, let's face it are a contrary lot) have developed their own Coronation by throwing the lavender gene into the mix. Their birds have pretty lavender neck wing and tail feathers instead of our grey, and they breed true.

And of course we had *Buffy the Wormslayer.*

Buffy was a lovely Buff Sussex bantam who had been the only one to hatch from a batch of posted eggs, and had grown up with three large fowl Speckled Sussex and thought she was one of them. She was incredibly tame and would hop onto my arm and stay there while I walked around visiting people on the allotments.

She would hop off and have a scratch around while I was chatting, and then come back when it was time to move on. Every time I tried to separate her from the big birds (I was terrified that the huge cock bird would try to mate with her when he was mature) she just pined away. The situation was only resolved when we travelled down to Kent to buy a handsome boyfriend for her, a magnificent Buff Sussex bantam lad. They set up home in our garden and raised several batches of chicks there, free ranging in amongst the shrubs and flowers.

Any Fool Can Be A.......

Buffy the Wormslayer's Diary became a regular and popular feature in the local poultry club's newsletter – a chicken's daily life, written from the point of view of the chicken. On reflection it was clearly a sign of impending madness.

Around this time I made a fantastic find on Ebay – a truly *superb* trailer. It is rather like the ones towed by juggernauts, having a steel framework superstructure that can be broken down if need be, with a tarpaulin cover over it.

German made, it has low steel side walls and floor and a dropdown tailgate and, as far as I know, nothing like it is available in the UK. It turned out that the guy selling it was a Dutchman who wanted to move to England but was quoted an astronomical price by a removals company, and so he bought the trailer to do the job himself. I watched the bidding, which was very hot - obviously plenty of others realised what a great buy it was. One guy in particular was very keen, instantly bidding back each time he was outbid. I made my move five seconds from the end of the auction and was delighted to secure it it for just over five hundred quid – an absolute bargain!

Then things got a little complicated as the seller wanted us to send payment immediately by Paypal, which is a system of paying electronically over the Internet and charging your credit card. It was still in its infancy here in the UK, although we had been using it for some time in the US by making use of an American friend's address. We couldn't collect the trailer for a few days and when we told the seller this he informed us that he was emigrating to Australia in two days, but if we sent the money he would arrange for his neighbour to hand over the trailer. Now I don't know about you, but I'm not keen on sending five hundred notes to somebody who isn't going to be around much longer and who won't want to know if there is something wrong with the trailer, or worse still there is no trailer! If I could set up a Paypal account using a fake address so could anybody else.

We traded increasingly niggly emails, until eventually I decided to change all our scheduled arrangements and pick the trailer up the next day and pay cash.

It turned out to be a good decision as the underbidder was very upset at not winning, and had offered the vendor considerably more money for it.

So we made an uneventful trip to Surrey and towed our trophy home. As things turned out it was the first of several trips to this county, and each time we would return with a splendid prize. The trailer was to prove to be worth its weight in gold.

Sheds - you can never have too many!

A friend contacted me as his mother had died and he had to clear her house. She had several sheds that I could have for free if I took them away.

We were round there like a shot!

We didn't take the new trailer as it wouldn't be big enough to fit the sheds inside, and the framework would take too long to dismantle. They could lie on top of the old smaller one though, and so that one would be fine.

We arrived to find a scene that looked like a bomb had landed! A skip in the driveway was rapidly filling up and the back garden was strewn with junk, debris and unidentifiable bits of this and that plus a few gems. My friend's mum's partner had been a hoarder on a *huge* scale and the numerous sheds were filled to the brim with all manner of things, as was the loft of the bungalow.

I was soon climbing into the skip to retrieve all manner of treasures that were way too useful to throw away and nearly cried when I was informed that this was the third skip they had filled. Rolls of wire, galvanised iron cages, old copper washing dollies, iron saucepans and heaps more goodies were piled into the trailer.

As for the sheds they were an allotment holder's dream! Most of them were too big or too difficult to dismantle. There was an old beach hut that I would dearly have loved to relieve him of, but it was just too big to get onto my trailer. This was a great shame as it was so strong it would have made an excellent secure tool store. In the end I settled for two identical 3′ x 3′ sheds that I felt would make great chicken houses. These were quickly dismantled and carried out to the waiting trailer, where we discovered that we had a problem. We had liberated so many goodies that we had filled the car and piled the trailer up so high that the sheds wouldn't lie flat on the top as planned. I realised that the shed sections would actually fit inside the trailer though, and so all the junk.....sorry.....useful bits and pieces were moved to one side to make space and the shed pieces stood vertically on their sides against the trailer side wall and securely lashed in place. It looked a bit odd, but it was the only way we could get all our loot home.

As we drove off and turned the first corner the whole lot swayed precariously but I knew that it was firmly attached to the side of the trailer. Our journey home involved a circuit of the Ipswich bypass, which took us over the huge Orwell Bridge. We drove round the last mini-roundabout and as we took the exit for the bridge the whole load yet again leaned with the turn......but this time there was a loud CRACK! and the whole lot tilted drunkenly to one side! A section of the trailer side wall had broken away and was leaning out into the next lane of traffic – with all the shed pieces lashed to it.

We had no option but to carry on and pray as there was very little that we could do. As we slowly approached the bridge, with me anxiously watching the shed in the rear view mirror, I realised that the main A14 beside us and ahead of us was empty, which was rather strange at this time of day. A glance in my mirrors gave me the reason – US! Nobody was prepared to pass us with our patently unsafe load teetering on the edge of total collapse, and we were building up a huge queue of traffic behind us stretching way back.

The Orwell Bridge rises very high across an open and exposed section of the River Orwell, and there is a wicked crosswind. As we slowly made our way across, leading our enormous convoy of cars and trucks, our load tipped repeatedly from one side to the other. Each time that it swayed out into the road we fully expected the whole lot to break away and land in the fast lane.

Any Fool Can Be A.......

There are police traffic cameras at intervals all along this road, and I will never understand how film of our escapade has never appeared on 'Police, Camera, Action!' or 'You've Been Framed!' We fully expected a set of blue flashing lights to come screaming up the hard shoulder, especially as Suffolk Police HQ was just up the road.

Despite all our fears the load somehow stayed attached to the trailer and was delivered to the allotments to join our growing collection of sheds. We had inherited a shed with each of three of the plots, built the Chicken Hilton and these two brought our total to six. You can never have enough sheds though!

One was quickly put to use as a chook house, while the other one was stored until I found a use for it – which I soon would, and would need another one as well.

Our switch to raising only bantams didn't work out too well. It was strange really because there are far more bantams exhibited at small local poultry shows than there are large fowl, and so we thought that we would be able to dispose of our spare pullets to a ready market. It didn't turn out that way at all and we really struggled to find buyers for our beautiful buff young girls. They really are so attractive and good natured, as well as making excellent mums, that we were amazed when nobody wanted them. We also found that the cock birds really didn't have enough meat on them for our needs. Don't get me wrong, they would make an excellent single meal for two or three people, but we like to have a Sunday roast, followed by cold meat on a Monday, and curried chicken later in the week.

Bantams produced only a very small portion for each, and I really didn't like ending the life of another creature for such a small reward. I've never really understood the killing of small songbirds to bake in pies, and in my eyes the bantams were a very similar proposition. We also found that people didn't want their eggs. Whilst large eggs always found a ready home, and the small amount of cash we received helped a little towards the cost of their feed, bantam eggs were a different case altogether. We ended up using all the bantam eggs ourselves, whilst letting other people have the large eggs.

So we switched back to large birds again, and regretted selling our lovely Red Sussex. They were a very good strain with huge cock birds. We knew this because we hatched eight chicks and every single one grew into a cock bird, and they were all a lovely size. They were big, strong birds though, and very difficult to kill efficiently. I had bought a hand-held dispatcher, a tool like a pair of pliers, which dislocates and breaks the bird's neck if used properly. It was good enough to deal with a bantam cleanly and quickly, but the thick, gristly neck of a big cock Sussex was a different matter.

I used it when I killed the last of the Red Sussex, hung the lad up by his legs in one of our numerous sheds and Sue helped me to pluck him. Our birds are always killed away from the sight and sound of the rest of the flock, and we had found it better to do the plucking indoors somewhere to prevent the whirlwind of feathers that you get if you try to do the job outside in even a slight breeze.

We were about half way through the job when he suddenly woke up and started squawking, and flapping his featherless wings! I hadn't managed to kill him, only throttled him into unconsciousness, and now he was being plucked alive.

We were absolutely mortified. A healthy and happy life followed by a quick and painless death was at the very heart of all that we were trying to achieve. After this sad experience we bought a heavy duty wall-mounted dispatcher which was much more efficient for big birds, and eventually I found somebody who showed me how to do the job by hand, although I have never been comfortable doing it this way.

The bantam experience wasn't a complete failure though, as we found out what wonderful mothers the Sussex bantams make. They are not at all fussy how many they raise, or even whose chicks they are. In fact they aren't even fussy about the eggs as we have found one studiously incubating a large round stone!

They are so good as foster mothers that we were able to devise a system of hatching and raising chicks that did away with the need for heat lamps and artificial rearing. We discovered it after we had had a couple of moderately unsuccessful hatchings. Two broody hens had only hatched a couple of chicks each and we couldn't afford to use housing space for two such small broods. Last thing at night I 'stole' the chicks from one of them and popped them under the other one with her own chicks. She woke up the next morning thinking that she had hatched a couple more eggs and was happy with her increased brood. The hen that had lost her chicks stayed broody, which was helped by a couple of eggs being popped under her, and when we had some more eggs hatch in the incubator a couple of days later she was given the resulting chicks and happily accepted them.

Groups of chicks being raised together have to be the same age or the slightly older ones may bully or even kill the younger ones, so being able to 'foster' small hatches like this can be really useful.

This new discovery allowed us to swing into a different hatching mode altogether.

We no longer needed to hand rear chicks and keep them warm, and we could make sure that we had a decent-sized hatch. Instead of having loads of small hatches on the go virtually all through the late winter and spring, with chicks of all ages in different houses, we could go for one or two bigger hatches and get our year's supply out of the way quickly and efficiently.

We now wait until we have two strongly broody hens, which doesn't usually happen until around Easter time, and we give them a couple of eggs to sit on and keep them happy. In the meantime we collect enough eggs from our chosen breed or colour variety. Once we have twenty eggs for the incubator and another four for the hens, we swing into action with the next phase. The incubator is fired up while we are collecting eggs, and we run it for a couple of days to check that the temperature is correct, before filling it with the eggs. At the same time we also replace the eggs under the sitting hens with four new ones so that their eggs and those in the incubator hatch on the same day.

As the eggs at home hatch, the chicks are transferred into a box with heat lamp, food and water and given time to get their strength back and recover from their arduous birth. Last thing at night they are taken over to the allotments and popped under their new mums, who then take over the job of raising them. The system works remarkably well for us and has taken a lot of the hard work out of raising new stock. It is amazing how many chicks a bantam can cope with and she will still try to cover them at night when they are older – even large fowl chicks that are nearly as big as she is!

Our chicken breeding took a step in a new direction when I was offered a large fowl Coronation cockerel. This variety is incredibly rare and only a few people have them throughout the UK. We had accidentally produced a new colour in amongst a hatch of our bantams – something that revelled in the wonderful name of a Splash Buff Coronation Sussex. She was a lovely honey colour with white hackles and tail feathers – very, very pretty indeed. Sadly she didn't live to breeding age as I was looking forward to trying to fix the colour. Her picture even made it to the front cover of a national poultry magazine, but that is another story for later. Our lives were heading off in so many directions at once that we sometimes thought we must be going mad – or M.A.D.

The Coro' cockerel belonged to a young lad who was another Sussex enthusiast, and the young chap had been drawn into the same trap as us – falling in love with the breed and being drawn to all the colours. He was now going to concentrate on his main love – Red Sussex. He had scoured the country to get the Coro' and had mated him with a particularly nice Light Sussex hen – that he had got from me! As we had obtained our initial Red Sussex from him it felt somehow incestuous, but we swapped all our birds back and he ended up with a really good stud of Red Sussex whilst we had the embryo of a Coronation flock – the cockerel plus 3 chicks a few days old. I use that term quite loosely though, as the cock was not a good specimen by any means. He was no spring chicken, if you will excuse the awful pun, was very small and *incredibly* bad tempered.

Once ensconced in his pen with some Light Sussex hens he claimed them as his wives in true chook style with no courtship and, with no concept of the word foreplay, he became very possessive towards them. Whenever I entered the pen he would come scuttling towards me very aggressively. I very quickly learned to keep an eye on where he was at all times and keep facing him after he attacked me from behind and caught me in the calf with a spur. As I have already said, he was no youngster and his spurs were long and lethal. Combine these with his nasty temper and it's a shame that cock fighting is illegal because we could have earned a fortune with him. Before I get inundated with complaints and accusations of being a cruel sadistic monster, that bit was a *joke!*

I really didn't fancy trying to cut off his spurs either as he probably would have taken out one of my eyes in exchange!

We came to an uneasy understanding, but in the meantime the chicks that we got with him grew up and fledged, and we discovered that we had another Coronation, the rest being Lights. Even better news came later as it turned out to be a pullet, although a small one. We raised a big batch of eggs sired by the Coro' cock, and we got another Coronation pullet from them. Things were looking up.

A change of diet

H ome grown chicken is very tasty, much more so than just about anything that you can buy.

However, just like that 25lb Christmas turkey that you are still eating at the end of January, you really can have more than enough of a good thing. Roast chicken on Sunday followed by chicken sandwiches for lunch on Monday, cold chicken salad Monday evening and chicken curry on Tuesday can begin to get a tad tedious. So we looked around for an alternative meat source and plumped for rabbits. We already had several rabbit hutches that we used as chicken broody coops so there would be no major outlay involved.

We tried to source a breeding pair of the giant rabbits that are true meat animals such as the New Zealand breed, but couldn't find any locally. Then I chanced upon an advert offering some young standard Rex rabbits not too far away for a reasonable price. The Rex are the utility breed of the rabbit world, offering a medium sized meat carcass whilst still being a suitable size for pets. We decided that we didn't mind waiting a little while for them to reach breeding age as rabbits mature very young anyway.

Any Fool Can Be A......

When I rang the lady who was advertising, I found that the rabbits were now a good bit older than stated in the advert. She had only managed to sell a few, and if we took them all we could have them for free. Now as you know, that magical word 'free' really does hit the spot for me, and we rapidly set off into the Suffolk countryside to have a look at them.

They turned out to be four boys and a girl. They were a black boy, a brown boy, and two boys and a girl in a gorgeous bluey grey colour.

Notice that word 'gorgeous.' I really should have thought it through a bit more, but of course in my enthusiasm all that I could think of was getting some rabbits and varying our diet. I could now kill chickens efficiently, so I was ready for anything.

We took our new livestock home and set them up in a couple of hutches in the garden, the bucks in one and the doe by herself in the other. They weren't quite old enough to breed yet, but we had done enough reading to know that all hell would break loose if the boys started fighting over her. Clearly we only needed one male, and the lovely black had already been chosen as the sole survivor.

Our daughter talked about our rabbits at work, and her boss said that she would like one as she was looking for a rabbit, so we sold her one of the blue males.

The rest of them continued to grow, and one day we decided that it was time to put one in the freezer.

I selected one of the other blue bucks and took him out of sight and sound of the others. I had a spring loaded blackjack, or cosh, that I had found years before in a house clearance, and it would be just perfect for doing the job.

I sat the rabbit down on top of our wheelie bin to get him at a comfortable height for me to deal with him. He stared back up at me trustingly through beautiful violet eyes.
I gulped and hesitated.

I hardened my heart. If I couldn't do this then I couldn't consider myself to be a smallholder.

I laid the cosh against the back of rabbit's neck, closed my eyes, took a deep breath, and swung the club with as much force as I could muster.

The rabbit gave one big convulsion and lay dead, and I felt awful.

Following the instructions in a book I removed the innards and hung it for a day or two, then expertly skinned it and dressed it.

We had rabbit casserole for dinner on the following Sunday. My mother and I both ate our portions and enjoyed them, but Sue and our son just pushed theirs around their plates.

In the end gave the rest of the rabbits away to family and friends as pets.....

Tunnel vision

I was absolutely determined to obtain a polytunnel, by hook or by crook, and continued to scour Ebay, the local papers and online adverts. Everything was either too much money, too far away or unsuitable for what we wanted.

Any Fool Can Be A.......

One day I spotted an advert for a net-covered 20´ tunnel for £75 being offered in Staines in Middlesex. It wasn't really big enough for what I wanted, and I wanted a plastic tunnel, so I decided against it.

The advert was there again the following week. We were waging a constant war against the pigeons that decided our cabbages and broccoli were not only very tasty but theirs for the taking, and I had to put wire netting around them and drape netting over the top to keep them away, so maybe a net tunnel wouldn't be a bad idea. I debated the pros and cons for a few days and then decided to go for it. I rang the number fully expecting the tunnel to be sold by now, but it was still available. I couldn't get over to Middlesex for a while so trustingly posted the sellers a cheque so that they would keep it for me.

I've always had great faith in the human race and believe that it is just a few who let us down, and my faith was rewarded this time when we eventually trundled over to Staines a couple of weeks later, dragging our trusty trailer with us. We used the airliners circling Heathrow Airport as a homing beacon.

In the moments of peace between planes roaring overhead the sellers explained that they had retired from a business selling pot plants. The tunnel was covered in shade netting and had been used to protect the plants from the sun.

The netting wasn't in the best of condition but they had made this clear when I rang them, and it was the frame that I was interested in. It turned out to be a fairly lightweight model with tubing about one inch in diameter, but it was a bargain at the price and I was very pleased with it.

We got it home and then had fun assembling it as it wasn't quite as straightforward as I imagined; pieces were not interchangeable and had to go in the correct places, but eventually I got the jigsaw pieces sorted and it was ready. We dragged the sections of shade netting over the frame and tied them into place.

Taking it down and reassembling it had not been kind to the netting; it had a lot of rips and tears, so I spent hours with a mattress needle and some nylon string cobbling it all back together. The netting was dark green, and the overall finished effect was somewhat like a camouflaged army nissen hut, but hey! We now had a tunnel!

I planted it out with all our brassicas and they did well in the shaded conditions. The pigeons couldn't get at them…but unfortunately the slugs could! The tunnel was in one corner of our plots with a heavily overgrown area beyond it, and the slimy thieves were coming in from there. We lost all the plants down that side but all the others thrived. Slug pellets stopped them from advancing any further, but I refuse to use slug bait out in the open because hedgehogs eat them and die a horrible death, but inside the tunnel, where neither birds nor hedgehogs can enter, I feel that they are safe to use.

The rear of the tunnel was sheltered by a large heap of compost that ran along the entire back perimeter of our plots. All the jungle-like growth that we had removed from the growing areas had been dumped here, and was rotting down nicely. I decided to plant our marrows along the ridge and added a couple of pumpkins too. We had grown some small pumpkins the previous year with great success, and so I thought a slighter larger variety this year would be good. I chose 'Big Max.'

So we had a tunnel, but it wasn't the one I wanted. The search continued.

In the meantime something dramatic happened that was to

change our lives forever and take us in a totally new direction, dragging us ever further into the M.A.D. world of downshifting.

Our finances really were in a mess. We had very little income and I was beginning to sell my possessions on Ebay to make ends meet. I had been an avid collector virtually all my life, starting with stamps when I was in primary school. Many varied collections had come and gone, but a lot of them were now stored in our attic and forgotten about. Our circumstances dictated that these should now be changed back into coins of the realm to help the cause, but something else was about to be unveiled that would help us.

I have already mentioned the ACL internet forum – that place has a lot to answer for as it is full of smallholders, wannabe smallholders and dreamers who fill your head with ideas. I was also drifting into other forums covering allotments, green issues, poultry, downshifting etc. It was in a poultry forum that I became great friends with the sub-editor of *Practical Poultry Magazine*, helping her to cope with the trials and tribulations that constitute running a forum. So many people seem to enjoy going into these places to cause trouble, and they either don't realise or don't care what distress they cause to people who are giving up their free time up to run the place. I have found that this happens in all areas of voluntary work and I am amazed that there are still people willing to put their sanity on the line to help others.

My support for this lady proved to have a very unexpected benefit for us and our dire economic situation, and I will never be able to thank her enough for the break that she gave me. I greatly believe that you get back pretty much what you give out, and the events that were about to unfold reinforced my belief in this belief.

We were chatting one day when she casually asked me if I could write a piece for the magazine. I was dumbfounded. I had always enjoyed writing and had edited several club newsletters over the years. Indeed, I had recently been talked into taking over the running of a local poultry club magazine. Of course I jumped at the idea, especially when I found out that I would be paid! The magazine planned their layouts for quite a few months ahead, so it would be some time before the article would be needed. We chatted some more over the next few weeks and she asked if I had any good photos of the chickens, or would I need to take some. I told her that there were a lot on our website, and asked her to take a look and see if they were good enough. I had started the site more as a diary for my own records than anything else, but a lot of people have been inspired by it over the years and we receive some wonderful emails.

She came back to me very quickly and was very excited by what she had seen. It turned out that she was also the sub-editor of another magazine, *Country Kitchen*, which specialised in cooking with seasonally available food and she wanted me to write about how we had become involved in the 'grow your own' movement.

I was only too happy to oblige and, in due course, a four page article appeared in the magazine featuring our allotments and with pictures of Sue and I included.

It gave us both a very peculiar feeling seeing ourselves in print. I had been pictured in the local papers several times and had even been on the radio (no, not in 'WANTED' posters, before you say it!), but this was a completely different league.

We had to include cooking recipes in the piece and take photographs of the finished article, which proved to be much harder than you would think. Getting the lighting, framing and angle just right is an art in itself and it sometimes took a hundred pictures before getting the one that was just right.

Any Fool Can Be A.......

The article was well received and the one-off piece suddenly developed into a series, with a lovely feature about us in the poultry magazine tucked into the middle of the run. Our unusual Splash Buff Sussex bantam and I were featured on the front cover. We were moving in new circles and new opportunities were opening up.

In the meantime my idea of using the compost heap to grow the marrows and pumpkins proved to be a good one, and they thrived. In fact, they thrived too well and they grew and grew.......and grew!

Big Max by name and Big Max by nature, the plants started spreading in all directions. They also started climbing up the net tunnel. I wasn't unduly worried as I had no idea what was coming. Our camouflaged nissen hut began to look very camouflaged indeed as the ever searching tendrils moved out into the roadway, out into our plots, over the leaf bin and out into neighbouring plots – in fact they moved out in all directions!

Worse was to come as the fruits began to form and big yellow beach balls began to appear all over the place. Yes, I know this is what we wanted to happen, but it was the size of these beach balls and their locations that were the problem. I suppose that the name 'Big Max' should have given us a clue as 'Big' means… well….BIG, and 'Max' also means….er….BIG!

The tendrils had now advanced twenty feet in all directions, scrambling over everything in their path, which of course included the net tunnel. As the fruits began to form we learned the true meaning of the word 'big' as the pumpkins grew ever larger.

The ACL forum had launched an online 'Biggest Pumpkin' competition, and for a laugh I entered it. Entrants had to measure the circumference of their biggest fruit and post the size

QUICK CALL 999, BIG MAX HAS BROKEN OUT!

online each week. When I measured ours I found that we were winning!

The problem was that fruits were forming everywhere, and I do mean *everywhere*. There were pumpkins in our leaf pen, pumpkins hanging from wire netting – and pumpkins suspended on our net tunnel. The entire top end of our allotments was buried in a twisted tangle of stems and tendrils, all covered with enormous leaves two feet across. We were now referring to them as our pet triffids, but like the original triffids they weren't tame as they were running wild with apparent designs on taking over!

Then the ones hanging on the tunnel began to grow.......the tunnel began to sag.........and as they grew some more, so the tunnel sagged some more.

The inevitable happened and I went to the allotments one morning to find a huge hole in the netting and pumpkins on the floor inside. The rotten netting had finally given up the ghost. Out came my needle and string once more and I sewed the net back together again, but it was beginning to look like a patchwork quilt.

And still the pumpkins grew.

We were way out in front of the main bulk of the contestants, but we had been joined by a late entrant who had obviously studied the field and weighed up his chances of winning before entering. He was a pumpkin enthusiast who was feeding his plants with a secret cocktail of growth promoting nutrients. Ours just got whatever they could suck out of the compost heap and that was it.

I understand that if you want a prize winning pumpkin you should trim off the lesser fruits so that all the growth goes into one Arnold Schwarzenegger of a fruit, but we didn't do that either – we were in this to grow food, not win prizes. The competition was fun, nothing more. Roast pumpkin, pumpkin pie and pumpkin soup were the important things.

As the closing date drew nearer the two of us were still way out ahead and it was clear that one of us would be the winner. The girth of our biggest pumpkin was an inch or two bigger than that of our rival, but I knew that this counted for nothing. The weather was changing and autumn was upon us, with the danger of frosts at any time. The top end of our allotments were littered with huge orange boulders everywhere, and I had caught somebody eyeing them up early one morning when he didn't realise I was about. As soon as he spotted me he cleared off quickly. We had also had an incident with unruly children clambering through the pumpkin patch and damaging stems, so we decided to bring in the harvest.

The competition was run on an honesty and trust basis, and to submit your final entrant all you had to do was pop it on some scales and take a picture of the weight reading. This proved easier said than done as all we had was a small set of bathroom scales, but eventually we managed to manoeuvre our giant cannon ball onto the platform and balance it there.

It weighed a very impressive 85lbs, which is towards the top end of what this variety can produce. What was even more amazing was the fact that we had another five pumpkins that weighed over 80lbs each, and a couple of dozen that were 50lbs or so – our compost heap had done us proud.

I posted the weighing picture on the ACL forum, and waited for two days for the closing date. What had started as a bit of fun had become quite an obsession – I wanted to win. Our rival posted daily updates of the circumference of his pumpkin, and it was growing by the minute. Things were looking bleak.

The big day came and we waited with bated breath to hear the size of the other pumpkin. I'm sure that we were being played with psychologically as the other leader waited until very late in the day to put up his results, and when he did it was quite remarkable.

His Atlantic Giant, which can grow to truly phenomenal sizes, had reached…….wait for it……exactly 85lbs!

It was a tie.

If we hadn't had to harvest our crop early we may have won outright, but it had been great fun and an interesting diversion from the slog of digging, hoeing and weeding.

But the daily slog was about to grow much greater as we were now irreversibly lost and going M.A.D.

A pig of an idea

Once upon a time nearly all folk living in villages kept a pig or two in the backyard. It was also very commonly done on allotments and many of the old boys on our allotments could remember them being kept until relatively recently on one of the fields in Ipswich.

Several people had suggested that I get pigs as we seemed to be doing the full 'Good Life' thing. "Tom and Barbara kept a pig in Surbiton, why don't you?" was a common cry. They insisted that it was still in the allotment rules that you could keep pigs.

Many of the smallholders on ACL had pigs, and when they described the wonderful taste of their juicy pork joints and sausages at slaughter time they made my mouth water. Our chicken was far superior to any of the shop bought chickens - it didn't taste like soggy cardboard, but had a succulent flavour and lovely texture – but even so was becoming a little tedious. There are only so many different ways you can cook a chicken.

Roast pork sounded very good and I could almost taste it as I thought about it.

I enquired amongst the other ACLers as to how much room was needed to raise a couple of pigs so that they enjoyed a good lifestyle. It appeared that our spare plot would be big enough, and that the pigs would even get rid of those damned fartychokes as they rooted around and ate anything that they dug up. We could even perhaps make their pen from the steel fence panels, and then move it onto another area when the pigs went to slaughter so that we manured our plots in rotation. It was beginning to look like a plan.

I spoke to the field secretary to see what his attitude would be to our new plans and he was very much in favour. He even suggested that we could possibly make use of a large overgrown area of the allotments, clearing it out and making it useable. This sounded like a cracking idea to me. Our plan was looking better by the minute.

I confidently made a telephone call to the local council, speaking to the lady in charge of the allotments throughout Ipswich and explained that I would like to apply for permission to keep some pigs on our field and that the field secretary was in favour as it would help him to reclaim some of the overgrown plots.

Her reply devastated me.

"I'm sorry, but we don't allow pigs on the allotments."

"But it says in the rules that we can keep them."

"They are the Allotment Holders Association rules, not the council rules."

I couldn't believe it. I patiently explained to the council official what we were trying to do. By now I was beginning to admit that we were going M.A.D., and that we were firmly headed down the road towards becoming as self-sufficient as possible. I pointed out that what we were doing was great publicity, not just for the allotments but also for Ipswich Council as we wrote about our adventures in a national magazine, but it fell on deaf ears. She was adamant that we could not keep pigs on allotments.

In spite of her opposition she was in fact very sympathetic to our cause and even offered to find me some spare council-owned land somewhere that I could rent on a short-term basis to keep livestock on. The reality, however, was that there would almost certainly be no water and it would be unfenced.

So it was back to the drawing board.

Our small orchard grew – well of course it grew; it consisted of trees! I mean, it got bigger. Yet another birthday had come and gone and when I was asked what I would like, I answered "Fruit trees, please." Pear, plum, cherry trees and a tayberry bush joined our four apple trees. I had pruned our redcurrant bush and stuck the cuttings in the ground around the base of the bush – four of them had rooted, and so we increased our stock but a gale blew our makeshift netting off the currant bushes, and by the time I spotted it the birds had stolen the entire crop. Our gooseberry bushes too were attacked by sawflies and stripped of their leaves. They didn't bear any fruit.

The carrotfly totally destroyed our carrot crop. The cauliflowers just rotted on their stems whilst still very small. Tom and Barbara never had these problems in Surbiton – everything always ended up rosy on the TV series.

The 'Good Life' wasn't all it was cracked up to be. It was turning out to be bloody hard work, but we persevered and fought the ongoing battle with the weeds and the pests.

We tasted our first ever asparagus and they were gorgeous, absolutely wonderful. We could only make a light picking, but we looked forward to future years with bigger crops as the crowns developed. We enjoyed lovely tender Brussel sprouts, picked so small they were only the size of broad beans, but they were so sweet. I had been a sprout hater all my life, but now I was a convert.

We discovered the joys of baked root vegetables and squashes, something we had never tasted. Beetroot, parsnips, butternut, pumpkin and celeriac were cut into chunks and spread on a baking tray, sprigs of rosemary and cloves of garlic added, then the whole lot baked together - superb. We learned the technique from Jamie Oliver. No, he didn't come round to see us; we watched his TV programmes like the rest of you.

The really weird bit for us was that our articles were appearing alongside his in the cooking magazine, as well as stories and tips from Hugh Fearnley-Whittingstall and Jimmy Doherty – people whose TV programmes we watched avidly. We felt as though we were rubbing shoulders with the stars.

I mentioned celeriac and I wonder how many of you have tasted it, or even know what it is? Do you remember years ago when a stick of celery was sold with a big knob of root still attached? As a boy I *loved* that bit! Nowadays it is nearly all trimmed off. Well *that* is exactly what the whole celeriac is like, a celery root.

It tastes wonderful eaten raw, and even nicer when baked. Oh, and if you leave it in the ground too long the carrot fly get it!

We managed to get another Coronation pullet from our breeding programme too. The genetics of this colour are such that you only get a tiny number of Coronations, the rest being normal Light Sussex. The size of the pullets was also improving, each one being slightly bigger than the last, as we were mating the original hens to our lovely big new Light Sussex Cockerel *Hagrid III*…or maybe IV, I've lost track.

We no longer had the Coronation cockerel to breed from. His aggressive behaviour had got worse and worse and he had taken to attacking me full-on as soon as I stepped into the run. A couple of times he had managed to creep up on me from behind and his spurs had injured me. He was such a bundle of fury that I really didn't fancy trimming his spurs, no matter how bad things got. Having him come charging across at me as soon as I stepped into the pen became very tiresome. I had been thinking about selling him and getting my money back, when one morning events took an unexpected turn.

I had filled the water drinker in their run and as I was returning with the feeder, I opened the shed door and was suddenly hit with great force on the back of my knee. It was a classic take-down and I collapsed in a heap on the floor of the run. Not the best place in the world to have a lie down, as you can imagine.

As I rolled over and tried to get up I did my best to ignore all the squidgy bits sticking to me, but I looked up and saw a pair of spurs hurtling towards my face. I'm afraid that the survival instinct kicked in, and I swung what I had in my hand to block the attack.

My hand was holding the metal feeder and I swung it just a little harder than I had perhaps intended.

Aggressive irate cockerel meets hard immovable object.
Aggressive irate cockerel sails backwards across the run.
Aggressive irate cockerel lands heavily and doesn't move.
Aggressive irate cockerel is a bit tough but tastes wonderful and is probably the most expensive chicken we have ever eaten!

We had his offspring though, and were slowly building up the small nucleus of a Coronation breeding flock.

Events suddenly took off in several different directions at once though, and life was about to get very busy indeed. We were finding that this 'Good Life' that everybody said we were living wasn't as good as it sounded – it really was damned hard work, and it was about to get a lot harder.

I was still scouring Ebay and the small ads for a polytunnel, and one day I spotted a newly-listed frame in the auctions with a starting bid of £50. Starting bids mean nothing in online auctions as everything happens in the last ten seconds with what are known as snipe bids. Rather than place their maximum bid early on, experienced buyers wait until the last possible second as this doesn't give other bidders a chance to run the price up. It means that inexperienced sellers think their item isn't selling, but it may suddenly get lots of bids and make a good price right at the very end.

This particular auction was very interesting as the frame was clearly being sold by somebody who didn't have a clue what it was, and it stated that the frame had to be collected by a certain date – which was the day after the auction closed.

I studied the pictures carefully and, as far as I could tell, the frame was complete but it was impossible to tell the size of the tunnel. It wasn't too far away though, so I emailed the seller and pointed out that it would be very difficult for a buyer to collect such a big item within 24 hours of the auction ending, and did they have a 'buy it now' price in mind as I could collect it straight away? A buy it now price means a figure that they are happy to sell at and will end the auction immediately.

The seller turned out to be a lady selling the frame on behalf of her uncle and she agreed that the collection timing could prove awkward, but it was cluttering up her space and she was moving ,so it had to go quickly. Would we like to make an offer?

Would we!

I replied, telling her that I had recently bought a frame for £75, and would be willing to pay the same for this one if that was acceptable.

She replied that she would accept £75 as she wanted it out of the way. We were in business!

We hurriedly set out for deepest, darkest Essex the next morning, complete with our trusty trailer, and when we arrived at the address it turned out to be a very nice farm. The lady vendor ran a furniture business from one of the barns, and the polytunnel frame was cluttering up one corner.

When I saw the frame I felt quite embarrassed as we had clearly got an absolute bargain. Our previous purchase had been a small lightweight frame, whereas this was obviously a different animal altogether – a heavy duty frame of indeterminate yet clearly very large proportions! To make matters worse (well, even better really, but you know what I mean) she said, "Would all these metal poles be of any use to you? You can have them for nothing if they are," and showed me a big heap of metal rods. It was a very old but clearly large fruit cage frame.

So we had 'stolen' a tunnel frame worth around £250 at least and we were now being offered a buy one get one free deal.

We drove home with me cock-a-hoop, and then set about organising the next stage of my plan.

Our writing for *Country Kitchen* magazine had come to an end, largely due to internal politics, I think. I was sad to lose this little bit of income, but it had been a hugely enjoyable experience and I had learned so much. Taking photographs to a high enough standard for publication is not easy as there are so many things to consider such as framing, light, angle etc, and I soon understood why professional photographers have their cameras set up to go off like machine guns with twenty shots per second or something similar. If you shoot enough pictures then hopefully one of them will be just perfect! People being photographed invariably seem to blink just as the shutter clicks, and chickens are determined to bend over and show you their bums. Nineteen of them will be posing beautifully, but number twenty will moon at you, or the cockerel will decide to take advantage of a very attractive number seventeen while she is distracted by the camera.

Cockerels have no concept of foreplay and their idea of 'love time' is when the hen is looking the other way and feeding. Muddy ground doesn't bother them either – after all it is the hen that gets squashed into the mud, not them. A waterlogged run will very quickly be full of very muddy hens and one squeaky clean cockerel.

I had noticed that a new magazine dedicated to the 'grow your own' fraternity was being launched. The editor was a member of the ACL community and I had contacted him to wish him good luck. He got back to me and asked me to write something for the new mag, which was to be called *Grow It!*

One door had closed and another had opened. I wrote a piece about secondhand polytunnels and the perils of buying them, which was accepted, and the payment more than covered the cost of the frame I had bought. A further article describing how to erect a used tunnel would help pay for the new plastic cover, which promised to be quite expensive.

The tunnel turned out to be a massive 42' x 15' and the building of the frame was incredibly hard work. The ground rods were rusted solid onto the hoops and no amount of penetrating oil or hammering would shift them. I had to work out a new system for building the frame as there were going to be no ground rods put in place first! Eventually I settled for hammering a scaffold pole into the ground to the desired depth, twisting it out, and then dropping the ground rod and half hoop into the hole provided. It took a lot of careful measuring and cross checking to ensure that the tunnel was straight and square, and I was delighted when the final hole was only one inch out of place.

The next part of my masterplan kicked in. I contacted tunnel manufacturers and explained that I would be writing an article for the magazine about re-covering a polytunnel and blatantly begged for a discount on the price of the plastic.

One company rewarded my bare-faced cheek with a big discount on the price of the cover and the necessary hotspot tape, and I was in business! A huge, very heavy roll of plastic arrived and the whole family were placed on standby to help as this was going to be a very big job, and in the meantime I got stuck into the *really* hard part of the job. In two days I dug out six tons of soil as I prepared the trenches into which I would need to sink the plastic into the ground all around the tunnel. One hundred and ten feet of trenches one foot wide and eighteen inches deep in rock hard sandy soil certainly helped my weight-reduction programme. They also helped my insomnia problem too, as I collapsed exhausted into bed each evening.

I quickly built and fitted the timber end frames as summer was rapidly fading and the weather was threatening to change. I prayed that we would get no heavy rain that might collapse the trenches dug in such sandy soil, and waited impatiently for a warm, still day to dawn. If you fit plastic on a cold day it will expand on a hot day and go baggy. Similarly, if it is too hot when fitted it will shrink on a cold day and be too tight. A windy day is the last thing you need when you are struggling with a huge piece a plastic that doubles wonderfully well as a huge sail and is likely to fly away, dragging you and all your helpers with it.

Finally a suitably promising day arrived and I set out to the allotments with my army of willing assistants. Sons, daughters and their spouses were all dragged along to help control the monster piece of plastic. The promise of photos in a magazine brought out the Gucci sunglasses and Prada bags – and the girls were even worse!

Amazingly the whole exercise went off remarkably well, which was undoubtedly due to my inspired leadership, and we had finished the whole thing by lunchtime.

All that remained was to make the end doors and then the tunnel would be complete. I wanted to build them with wooden frames and plastic net meshing so that butterflies, birds etc. could be kept out and plenty of air could get in for ventilation and small bugs to pollinate the crops.

When I went into the allotments the next morning to feed the chickens I couldn't help but stop to admire my lovely tunnel. From a distance it looked wonderful and dominated the allotments. I found that a stupid pigeon had wandered into the tunnel and couldn't find his way out again. As I chased him out I thought to myself that the netting doors were certainly a good idea, and that I needed to get them built and hung before I could start planting or this plump pigeon get even plumper at my expense.

The article I wrote for the magazine turned out to be a huge success and was serialised over two issues. The payment more than covered the cost of the cover, so I had a lovely tunnel that had not only paid for itself, but had actually shown a profit! This was frugal living on a scale I hadn't believed possible.

I was even more proud later when I found that the polytunnel company had asked for permission to use my article to show people how to build a secondhand tunnel, and the whole thing could be downloaded from their website.

However, disaster was lurking just around the corner........

Things get a little M.A.D.

I was chatting to the field secretary one morning and he seemed in a good mood, so I thought that I would chance my arm and ask again about pigs – could he think of any way of persuading the council to allow me to have them?

He said that he couldn't see it happening as since swine fever, foot and mouth etc. the council had taken a hard line over pigs in public places. Seeing my forlorn and crestfallen look, he casually added, ".....but you could ask about goats."

I was totally amazed, and very excited. This could mean milk.... butter....even cheese!

A whole new world of possibilities opened up in my head. I was very afraid of being disappointed again, but he reassured me that the council would definitely give permission for goats.

I dashed home to tell Sue, who was profoundly unimpressed. I would obviously have to work on her.....

A couple of mornings after the Great Grand Polytunnel Building Day I unlocked the allotment gates and glanced across to admire the tunnel again. This was already becoming a morning ritual. I was so proud of the tunnel and it looked so good, but this morning something didn't look quite right. I couldn't put my finger on it, but something was amiss.

As I got a bit nearer I realised that the tunnel had a brown sheen to it. Somebody had been throwing mud at my beautiful tunnel!

No, that still wasn't it. There was clearly dirt on the plastic, but it was in streaks and spots.
When I entered the tunnel I was completely bewildered. The whole of the central roofline from one end to the other was covered in muddy footprints, and there were several areas where they went up the side walls too. Closer inspection showed that things were even worse though, because everywhere there was mud there were also holes. The whole tunnel was a massive pincushion of claw holes. The roof was bad enough, but the damage to the sides was even worse where the creature had dragged itself up the sheer walls by hooking its claws into the plastic.

I was devastated. So much hard work had gone into finding and building the tunnel. To have it damaged so badly, and so quickly, was heartbreaking.

The holes were made by thick, blunt claws so it couldn't have been a cat, and anyway the creature's paws were far too big. Closer examination showed two different sizes of pad marks, and they didn't match a dog's paws either. I should have immediately realised the culprits, but it took some Internet research on animal paw prints before I realised that the tunnel had been attacked by our arch enemy – foxes! Just to add insult to injury, we had been visited by both mummy and daddy fox as the marks belonged to a fox and a vixen.

I contacted both the tunnel company and the magazine editor – it was a new one on them; neither had ever heard of a tunnel being attacked by foxes before.

Nobody could come up with a credible reason as to why the foxes would do it either. It was bizarre. Then I remembered the pigeon that had been trapped inside the tunnel. If something else had got in and was flying around, the foxes wouldn't be able to resist it and would chase it from end to end and keep jumping up and down to try to catch it.

I ordered some repair tape, washed the tunnel down with a hose and scrubbed it with a long-handled broom. I also resolved to make and fit those end doors as soon as possible.

Meantime Sue was ordering goat books from the library, which was a good sign.

A neighbour on the allotments had a relation who ran a hire company leasing out construction site fence panels and he sold off slightly damaged ones. I placed an order for six panels for a goat pen. There's nothing like optimism is there? They could always be used for another chook run if things didn't work out. When I returned to the allotments the next morning I found yet more damage. This time the foxes had been back on the polytunnel roof and they seemed to have found a nail file from somewhere and sharpened their claws nicely as there were yet more rips and holes.

I cancelled what I had planned to do that day and visited the local DIY store to buy timber for the tunnel doors. I dug out the birdproof netting from the loft that I had bought in case of a bird flu epidemic and used some of it on the door frames. The tunnel now had doors at either end that kept out birds, butterflies and cats, but would let in plenty of fresh air.

No, I will modify that statement – the doors let in some fresh air. If I were building the tunnel again, the only thing I would change would be to install full width double doors instead of a normal-sized single door. As soon as the sun rises in the morning the tunnel starts to heat up and I swear the temperature in there regularly goes over one hundred degrees. It is impossible to work in there for more than a few minutes at a time during the heat of the day before rushing out gasping for some air and a cool breeze. Anybody wanting to lose weight is cordially invited to come and work in my polytunnel for a couple of hours!

All this is by the by; I now had doors fitted to stop birds entering, which I thought were attracting the foxes.
It didn't work.

The foxes had now clearly established a quick stomp on the roof as part of their nightly routine and the next morning there was clear evidence that they had organised a full blown rave overnight. Muddy footprints were everywhere and hundreds more claw holes had appeared. By now I was at the end of my tether and concerned about the structural integrity of the tunnel covering. The plastic was so weakened in places that I was seriously worried about what would happen when the first gales struck.

The crows were also now joining in with the party spirit. Myriads of insects were getting trapped in the tunnel and gathering in droves inside the top of the roof, squeezing in between the plastic and the metal hoops. The crows could see them and obviously thought lunch was being served. They were now pecking holes through the plastic to get to them, and some of the holes were *big!*

Patching them with repair tape was almost impossible. To be effective the tape has to be applied to both sides of the plastic. The frame was in the way on the inside and, whilst the foxes could easily climb onto the roof, I couldn't. The crows eventually got bored with their attempts to get an easy insect breakfast, but to this day the tunnel remains self-watering along the ridge lines.

My poor tunnel was only a week or so old, but it now looked like it was covered in bandages as there was so much repair tape stuck all over it.

The only thing that I could think to do now was to build a wall around the tunnel. In amongst the piles of spare bits and pieces that I had stacked here and there – cheap auction purchases, or stuff discarded by other allotment holders that I thought 'might come in handy sometime' – I had a hundred feet of four foot high chainlink fencing. I hammered makeshift metal posts in down both sides of the tunnel and attached the fencing. The tunnel now began to look like Stalag 5 – all it needed was some machine gun posts and searchlight towers.

And *still* the foxes came that night! The fence on one side was a little further away from the tunnel wall, but the foxes were jumping it and getting into the gap before climbing up the tunnel wall.

In desperation I spread plastic netting along the whole length of the top of the fence. It worked. Peace reigned once more.

Each morning I apprehensively checked the roof to see if any more new paw prints had appeared overnight, but all was quiet on the Polytunnel Front.

Life began to return to normal and I began planting in the tunnel. As it was late in the season there wasn't too much I could get on with, but I planted up a whole load of spring cauliflowers that I hoped would get us through the 'hungry gap.'

One morning when I went into the tunnel to water, I noticed a wet patch on the floor. Looking up I was horrified to discover a three inch wide hole in the roof! How it had appeared was a mystery, but out came the repair tape once more.

The next morning a new and huge hole appeared in one end next to the door I had fitted.

By now I was feeling suicidal! There were no signs to give me a clue as to what had caused this fresh damage, apart from pieces of shredded plastic strewn around. Soon we would have spent more on tape than we had saved on the new cover, not to mention having more tape than polythene covering our new tunnel!

The next morning it was the turn of the other end, again at ground level as another big hole appeared with yet more shredded plastic strewn around and footprints.

Well, not footprints exactly, but tiny paw prints. And teeth marks around the edge of the hole. Teeth marks made with two large front incisors.

We now had squirrels joining in with the 'Wreck a Poly Party.'

I hastily scanned the pages of my favourite website - Ebay – and purchased a live squirrel/rat trap for next day delivery, and as soon as it arrived I scuttled across to the allotments and set it next to the tunnel, baited with peanuts. The field secretary ws on record as having caught seventeen squirrels in the last few months on his plots across the other side of the field, so I was quite hopeful of catching the culprit.

Every morning I checked the trap but it was empty – literally. The mice had probably been enjoying the peanuts, but there was no sign of a squirrel. They weren't attacking the tunnel any more either. The weather had changed for the worse by now, so I eventually concluded that the polytunnel demolition crew was now hibernating.

Early the following spring a minibus turned up on the allotments one Sunday morning (not with more squirrels, thankfully!) and a crowd of teenagers and older men all wearing bright yellow jackets climbed out. They were handed heavy duty petrol strimmers and other tools, and they set to hacking away at the huge jungle of eight feet high brambles that covered about eight abandoned plots and stretched to the perimeter fence.

Over the next few days the whole area was cleared and the debris burned, and it turned out that the guys in yellow coats were petty criminals condemned to doing hours of community service by the local courts. We all checked that our shed padlocks were in good working order.

When they had finished slashing and burning a council tractor arrived and ploughed out the bramble roots, after which the plots were very quickly shared out amongst those on the waiting list. Growing your own was now becoming fashionable again
.

Civilisation had also returned to foxearth corner, and the foxes had been evicted. We had no further attacks on the polytunnel, but the wildlife hadn't finished with us just yet, oh no.

Acting the goat

Our adventures with animals were only just beginning.

I had telephoned the council lady again, this time to ask for permission to keep goats on our plots. After a long pause she replied, "Oh dear, I only recently turned down a nice chap who wanted to keep pigs. I'm not at all sure that I can let you have goats."

When I assured her that the nice chap had in fact been me she was very relieved and gave me permission to keep some goats on a twelve month trial basis. I would be responsible for any damage they did and the situation would be reviewed.

Our search for goats did, however, proved to be a very long and frustrating one.

Things got off to a good start when my brother-in-law offered me a shed that would be big enough for a goat house. An 8´ x 6´ shed would be ideal. The fact that it was fifty miles away was a minor detail as we were now experienced shed shifters. I bought a big reel of very thick nylon rope and we headed off to Essex. When we arrived I was surprised by just how *big* an 8´ x 6´ shed is! The panels seemed enormous and our trailer very small.

We laid them flat on the trailer, bridging across the tops of the walls and they stacked quite high, which was a little worrying, but we lashed them tightly in place. I didn't fully trust the cleats that I had screwed to the sides of the trailer as one had snapped previously, so I ran our thick nylon rope right under the trailer and out the other side, taking it back over the top. I did this a few times from side to side and back to front, and tied the whole thing very securely. We had learned from our hair-raising ride over the Orwell Bridge and this shed wasn't going anywhere except to our allotment!

We set off home and as we turned the first corner the trailer swayed drunkenly to one side and then straightened. It repeated this motion all the way home every time we swerved or turned. The trailer had very good suspension, and we had effectively raised the centre of gravity a lot by piling it so high with heavy panels, hence the wild swaying. Once I had convinced myself that the trailer wasn't going to overturn I couldn't watch it in the rear view mirror any more as it made me feel seasick.

Any Fool Can Be A.......

At one point we were passed by a police car and my heart nearly stopped. They drove past very slowly whilst the co-driver ran his eye all over the trailer and its load, but he obviously decided it was a safe load and they sped off. I did wonder whether Suffolk Police had put out an APB to all local forces, warning them that there were shed-towing nutters loose in the area.......

The shed proved to be in poorer condition than it appeared with a lot of rotten sections, and it was difficult to re-erect. The roof, in particular, was hard to make secure and I had visions of the goats having plenty of ventilation if we ever had severe gales.

I managed to acquire some more steel fence panels and built a 22′ x 22′ pen surrounding the shed. We were just about ready for the goats, but we just couldn't find any.

We had narrowed down our choice of breed to Toggenburgs or Anglo-Nubians, but both would probably produce far more milk than we could use.

The Suffolk Smallholders' Society had a talk planned, but as it coincided with a visit from an American friend we thought we would have to give it a miss. We were very disappointed as nothing beats talking to experienced people when you are a beginner.

I had met Dave years before through the Internet, and we had got to know each other well, but had never met. He had been very kind to me, acting as a US agent when I went on collectable buying sprees, shipping them to him from all over the States, and he would pack them all into one huge box and send them on to me. A hard-nosed businessman, he humoured the mad Brits who were living like medieval peasants and was convinced that he was visiting a backward country.

We tossed good-natured abuse at each other non-stop.

I had never even seen a photo of him, so when I met him at Heathrow I was faced with an identification problem. I decided that I would need a sign to catch his attention, and after a lot of thought I set off to the airport suitably equipped.

The arrival gate opened onto a long, fenced off greeting area, lined on both sides by people holding up signs like 'Mr. Smith from Boston' or 'Mr. Brown from Kansas.'
I began to wonder if my sign was such a good idea.

I stood as close as possible to the gate and held up my sign. New arrivals began to exit and they all laughed or smiled when they saw my sign. People waiting beside me asked what was on the sign, and when I showed it to them they burst out laughing. An old man who had just arrived hobbled up to me and said, "Hey buddy, will I do?"

Curiosity was spreading along the line of waiting people, and I was getting shouted at to show them my sign. When I did, the laughter spread far and wide.

A guy who had just arrived tapped me on the shoulder and said, "Hi Mike, nice to meet you at last......I think! Nice sign."
The sign? Oh yes.

HELLO OLD FART
WELCOME TO THE
THIRD WORLD

And so Dave descended upon us, a chain-smoking New Yorker who we soon discovered existed on cigarettes, coffee and little else. In typical tourist style he arrived festooned with cameras (although he was an ex-press photographer so he had an excuse) and wanted to take shots of everything including the allotments, so that he could show the folks back home how these strange

Any Fool Can Be A.......

Brits lived.

The chickens, beans and tomatoes were photographed from every conceivable angle, and then we reached the new goat enclosure. "Hey, what's this shack doing in a prison compound?" enquired the Yank.

I explained that it was his sleeping arrangements.
Between snapshots I told him the real reason for the shed and run and he was incredulous.

"You want to keep *goats*?"

I explained the benefits of goats – eating all our unwanted vegetables, giving milk and providing a welcome change from chicken meat.

"You want to *eat* goats?"
I explained that the idea was to breed them and eat any male kids, and told him that there was a smallholders meeting about goats that evening, but obviously we wouldn't be going now.
"Oh yes we will – I want to hear about these goats."

Hmmm. OK. I didn't tell him that there was no smoking allowed.

We duly arrived at a village hall in the middle of nowhere as people began to turn up from far and wide. This was obviously a popular subject as there was a good turnout. Around fifty people attended, which was much higher than normal.

Dave turned to me and asked, "Do all these folks keep animals and grow stuff?" He shook his head in bewilderment when I told him that they did.

Julie, who was giving the talk, set up boards with lots of photos on them and started to explain to us all the facts about raising goats.

Dave sat at the back with his arms folded and very quickly began to look bored. Occasionally he turned to me and raised a quizzical eyebrow.

Eventually he turned to me again.

"How long will this last?"

"Oh, about two hours."

Dave stared moodily at the 'NO SMOKING' sign and began to fidget.

The rest of us were totally enthralled by the talk.
Eventually Julie ran out of words and invited us all to look at the photographs. Cups of tea would be served and we could ask questions. As the audience moved forward to see the pictures I turned to speak to Dave but there was no sign of him.

Smoke drifted in through the door as Dave managed to get through most of his packet of cigarettes during the ten minute interval.

Julie kept Golden Guernsey goats and had two young girls and a billy with a most impressive spread of horns. They were absolutely gorgeous...really beautiful creatures. They were only of a moderate size too (which pleased Sue) and they gave a good amount of milk, but not so much that we would drown in it, and importantly they had gentle natures.

Dave reappeared.

Any Fool Can Be A.......

"Well I guess that little talk put you off of keeping goats, eh?"

"No"

"You *still* want to keep them?" Dave asked incredulously.

Julie's goats looked so lovely in the photographs that, while Dave was outside having another fag, we asked her if we could go to see them. She was more than willing and we arranged a visit for the next day. When Dave returned we informed him that he would be making a house call on some goats the following day.

He suddenly felt the need for another smoke and dashed outside mumbling something about having only been in the country a few hours and already he knew more about goats than the whole of the rest of the citizens of the US put together.

The following afternoon we drove into deepest Suffolk to visit Julie and her Golden Guernseys. She lived near Framlingham, so we offered to take the Yank to Framlingham Castle for a look-see, but he wasn't interested. I have a theory about this: everything in America is bigger, better, older, newer, more expensive, less expensive or even bigger *and* less expensive than in the UK – at least it is according to Americans. They don't have any real history though, hence no castles, so they can't say theirs are better. Either that or they simply can't count back beyond two hundred years.....

When we arrived at Julie's Dave elected to stay with the car. I knew this was so he could smoke some more, but Suffolk is too nice to be polluted, so he was dragged along with us to see the goats.

As we walked round the back of the barns a most peculiar musky smell made our nostrils tingle.

Julie led us into a stable and there we met two lovely young girls who were equally pleased to see us. When Sue and I entered their pen they crowded round us looking for some love and attention. Oh, don't be silly, they were goats – they crowded round us looking for FOOD! Dave was invited into the pen to come and say hello too, but he stayed resolutely outside. I think he was afraid that the goats would eat his dwindling supply of cigarettes.

Golden Guernsey goats are quite well named as they come from Guernsey and are golden. Well, most of them are, or a lot of them are. Actually, some of them are. They range from a lovely deep auburn/chestnut colour to a sandy golden shade, and they have long flowing coats. Well most of them do, or some of them.

Actually, they range from long haired blonde types to quite short haired auburn jobbies......but they are definitely gorgeous.

We were hooked. Even Sue agreed that they were the ones for us. Dave just only prepared to agreed that we were M.A.D.

Julie offered to take us to see Peter. As we approached another stable that strange musky smell got much stronger. Julie opened a door and the smell hit us in huge great waves as Peter was revealed in all his glory. Her two girls were of the auburn medium coated variety and dehorned, but Peter was a long coated blonde with a phenomenal pair of horns which, instead of curving backwards, arced out sideways. I have no idea how Julie got him through the doorway into the stable – with a shoehorn, possibly. Dave took one look and returned to the car, grasping for his cigarettes.

When we commented on the smell Julie said, "Oh, does he smell? I hadn't noticed. He actually smells much stronger in the breeding season."

Billies secrete this scent from glands behind their ears and will rub themselves over anything nearby to mark their territory. They will mark their females, their pens, gateposts – and you! The theory is that they need to smell strongly in the wild to attract females to their wilderness habitats. They obviously don't consider this musky smell to be strong enough as they top it up by peeing all over themselves and rolling in anything strong smelling. I think I know one or two humans who must be related to goats....you know, the ones you sometimes find yourself next to in queues or see on Saturday nights rolling in the gutter, drunk.

Poor old billies live very lonely lives. Very few people keep them and most people send them to slaughter at about six months old. More enlightened owners give them a castrated male as a companion, but many live alone for as much as fifty weeks of the year, only having company when the girls come into season.

We decided that we couldn't keep a billy on the allotments – although the smell probably would have kept trespassers and vandals at bay. We simply couldn't afford to feed such an unproductive animal. Ours all have to earn their keep.

The search was now on for a couple of GG girls. It was going to be a long and frustrating search. In the meantime, normal life continued on the plots.

Our small flock of large fowl Coronation Sussex grew slowly. We moved the net tunnel and re-covered it with some of the nylon netting of which we had so much, and even managed to construct a lean-to annexe for it that gave us even more protected growing space.

Our writing suddenly came to a dramatic end when both our friends left their respective magazines after in-house restructuring. We hadn't earned much from the writing, but when you are earning very little in total every little contribution helps.

It had been a wonderful experience though, and of course we now had our magnificent (if somewhat war torn) polytunnel to show for it. Without the articles about the polytunnel we probably couldn't have afforded to buy it.

The searchers

No, we didn't meet the 1960s pop group and nor did we join John Wayne in his 1956 search for his young niece who had been kidnapped by Indians, but we did become the searchers, and our quest became well known as word travelled ahead of us.

I started contacting various goat groups and societies trying to find a couple of nannies. I hadn't realised just what a difficult job this would be, or how rare Golden Guernsey goats are. GGs nearly died out during the wartime occupation of the Channel Islands and only three distinct bloodlines survive. On reflection, and with the benefit of hindsight, there are probably a lot more non-pedigree GGs out there than most people realise, but as far as the societies are concerned they are not true GGs unless registered and their ancestry known. We wanted GGs and so we went down the conventional route. If we were starting again now I think that we would be content to get thoroughbred GGs for their size, temperament and milk production levels and wouldn't worry about that little piece of card from the British Goat Society.

We also made it much harder for ourselves because we did not want de-horned goats. Most goat breeders have their female goats de-horned virtually from birth. We considered it to be a slightly barbaric practice, and it totally goes against the ethos of why we grow our own and raise our own livestock. We want our animals to have the best possible life, and then a quick, clean death. De-horning is a traumatic and painful experience for a young kid and one that they sometimes don't survive. The horn buds are literally burned out. Although they are anaesthetised for the de-horning, it must be incredibly painful afterwards. We were not prepared to put any kids that we bred through it, and as you mustn't mix horned and de-horned animals, we had no choice but to look for horned adults.

We also didn't realise that breeders rarely sell adult goats, usually only parting with goatlings of about six months or so. We would have to wait something like two years to get any milk if we bought goatlings.

Finally, we didn't realise that we would come up against such a wall of hostility towards keeping goats on allotments. I know that some allotments are just an open area that the public can wander through at will and do more or less as they please, and that some have no water supply. Ours, however, are surrounded by high chainlink fencing topped with barbed wire and have heavy steel gates which are strongly padlocked. Trespassers are very rare and with the goats locked inside their shed, itself inside a secure pen, we felt that they would be perfectly safe and told everybody so. I had learned everything I possibly could about goats so that I could answer questions knowledgably and show that I knew what I was letting myself (and possibly others) in for.

But it made no difference.

Nobody had any goats for sale and nobody was prepared to put us on a waiting list. Even when we expanded our search to other breeds it was the same story. The only goats we were offered always had something wrong with them like a third teat, or one missing. It was OK to palm us off with their rubbish, but not to offer us any quality stock. One lady that I rang said as soon as she answered the phone, "Ah yes, you're those people that want to keep goats on an allotment, aren't you?" and didn't want to know. The jungle drums had obviously been beating. All this when we had heard that one of the top British Goat Society officials kept his goats on allotments!

There were one or two notable exceptions to this behaviour. One lady, Jill, was very supportive of us and really tried to locate some goats. She called me regularly and offered hours of advice. The stock officer of the Golden Guernsey Goat Society was also very helpful once he had satisfied himself that we were genuine. However, there simply weren't any goats available.

Even more frustratingly, one or two places in Wales that advertised GGs as being for sale didn't even reply to emails or telephone messages. Wales would have been a very long haul to fetch them, but we had reached desperation point.

It wasn't our own discomfort for such a long journey that we were worried about, purely the welfare of the goats. They didn't reply though, so the issue never arose. As it turned out much later this was very lucky for us.

One evening we took a phone call from Jill telling us that she had two young nannies coming in that may well suit us. They were crossbreeds but were the right sort of size for us. We were so excited as we put the finishing touches to their new accommodation. The goats duly arrived at our friends and were given a few days to settle down from their journey before moving on to us.

Then we received a sad telephone call from her. She had caught the goats up to put them into a pen so as to be ready for us to collect, and had given them a thorough once-over. They both had three teats! She had sent them to slaughter, and so our search was on again.

Any Fool Can Be A.......

Just when we thought that we would never be successful in finding some GGs we had a message from a lady in Surrey on the ACL forum: she was cutting down the numbers of her livestock and wondered if we would be interested in a two year old GG nanny and her one year old daughter?

WOULD WE?

Too right we would!

The electronic airwaves between Suffolk and Surrey became red hot with the number of messages flying backwards and forwards. I was concerned that we might not be able to afford them, but she assured me that a good home was more important than any price and that she would like us to have them as she had been following our frustrated search through the pages of the ACL forum. She was also looking for some bantam chickens and was interested in our small flock of Buff Sussex bantams, which we had decided to sell. Her goat price, reduced by the price of the bantams, came to a figure that we could comfortably afford and so it looked like we would finally get our goats.

I was a little concerned that our new trailer might not be suitable for collecting them, and I spoke to several people to see what they thought.

This superb trailer is of steel construction and has a drop down tail gate, but no livestock ramp so animals would have to be lifted into it. The low side walls are topped by a steel framework covered by a tarpaulin cover and a drop-down back sheet. The framework and cover can be removed if you need a flat trailer, but it is a big job. The steel floor has a raised, ribbed surface to help with grip. The whole thing looks like a miniature version of the forty foot trailers towed by huge HGV trucks. There is no ventilation, but the trailer holds a big volume of air. Everybody agreed that it would be fine to use for the goats unless it was a very hot day.

The big day dawned and it was bright but cool, so we set out for Surrey yet again with our hearts in our mouths and a load of chickens clucking away in the back of the car. It seemed hard to believe that we were at last coming to the end of our search.

When we arrived we were met by the lady and her daughter, who had her arm in a sling having broken her arm after a fall from her horse, and several excited dogs. We were also met by a row of goats standing along the rail of their paddock, looking at us speculatively to see if we were carrying anything edible. We were soon to realise that this is standard goat procedure, and that anything you are carrying, or indeed wearing, is likely to be tested for edibleness.

There was a beautiful big long haired blonde boy (who surprisingly didn't smell too bad at all), a very small goatling whose mother had apparently died after eating poisonous yew, and our nanny and her daughter and son. The seller did her best to persuade us to take the young boy too, but we were adamant that we didn't want him – he was after all directly related to both our females and so we couldn't use him for breeding. In the end she decided to have him castrated and she would keep him as a companion animal for the young goatling. The big billy didn't belong to her and would be going back to his owner.

Our mother goat was rather thin and the owner explained that she had accidentally gotten pregnant (the goat, not the owner) when she was only one year old, so the kids had taken a lot out of her. The smallholding had several large paddocks and we felt a little bit bad that the girls would be going into a fairly small pen, but we were going to make up for it by feeding them loads of fruit and veg and gathering branches. As goats are four legged eating machines they should be quite happy.

Any Fool Can Be A.......

The goats were easily enticed to the back of the trailer with....you guessed it already....food. We quickly learned that they would do anything for some brown bread – well the mother would, and she climbed into the trailer following some bread. Junior had to be bodily lifted into the trailer to join mum. Our chickens were introduced to their new accommodation and the deal was finalised.

So, armed with a couple of bales of straw and a bag of their usual feed, we set off on an interesting journey home. Every time we were forced to stop by red lights, roundabouts etc. the girls would let us know that they were still there.

There we were sitting amidst a load of traffic in West London, staring straight ahead at the traffic lights and pretending it was nothing to do with us, whilst all the people in the cars around us were looking around quizzically trying to figure out where the loud BAAAAAAAAing was coming from. If you were in London in June 2007 and were confused by an apparent ghostly flock of sheep, you now know the answer.

We stopped several times on the way home to check on the girls and to offer them food and, more importantly, water, but they just stared at us haughtily. They stood for the whole journey home, refusing to settle down. They were clearly nervous though, and their nerves had affected their bladders. The trailer was awash. If you were driving down the A12 in June 2007 and had your paintwork damaged by uric acid, it was nothing to do with us.......

We arrived on the allotments without incident and the goats were unloaded and led into their new accommodation. They immediately set to with gusto on the vegetation, totally ignoring us. In just four days four hundred square feet of two foot high grass and assorted weeds were reduced to about two inches. We had no idea that they could eat so much.

Our mother goat had a fancy Latin registered name but the youngster hadn't yet been registered. It had transpired during negotiations that our lady vendor wasn't in fact the owner and the goats actually belonged to somebody else, but we had been assured that he was quite happy with the sale and would register the goatling and then transfer the ownership over to us. No timescale was mentioned, however, and it took over six months and a lot of hassling from ourselves and other people before the girls finally became ours and we had the paperwork to prove it.

They had both been given pet names by their previous owner, but there was no way that I was going to be calling out 'Bambi' on the allotments, and so they were both immediately re-christened. The mother became Gertie and her daughter was Rosie. Gertrude and

Any Fool Can Be A.......

Rosetta were Sue's grandmother's middle names, and Gertie and Rosie sounded more like livestock names than Bambi.

Whilst they were in Surrey the girls were pets, but now they would have to earn their keep.

I built them an adventure playground out of old pallets with piles at different levels and they loved them. We soon discovered why you must not mix horned and de-horned goats as they joust enthusiastically all the time. By 'joust' I mean that they both rear up on their back legs and then bring their head (and horns) sharply down at one another with a tremendous CRACK! If only one of them had horns then there would certainly be a serious injury. The fighting scared the bejesus out of us to start with, until we found out from other goat keepers that it is quite normal.

They fought over the highest pile of pallets, so I levelled them off. It made no difference. They just constantly tested each other's strength. I don't think there was any real malice to it; it was just what goats do.

Gertie hadn't been milked and so her supply had dried up, which was a shame.

Until they had been mated and kidded we would have to feed them both with no return. We needed to mate them as soon as possible, but we would have to wait until they came into season. In the meantime I rang Julie, the lady who had given the goat talk at the smallholder's' meeting to see if I could make use of the services of her billy, Peter, when the time arrived.

Bad news - Julie had sold Peter to a rare breeds farm.

We began another search for goats and again found the same wall of discrimination against keeping goats on allotments. We also discovered that very few people actually keep billies!

One aspect of the goats that we hadn't known about was the need to feed them twice a day. All our interrogation of other goat keepers hadn't uncovered this fact. Most had said that you have to *milk* them twice a day, but nobody mentioned feeding twice. This meant that no matter what we were doing throughout the day, we had to be back in time to feed the goats and put them to bed. This was easier to do in the summer than the winter – especially difficult when it gets dark at 4.00pm. I solved this problem by buying a wind-up lantern. A few minutes of brisk handle turning and it would be charged up for half an hour or so, giving plenty of time for the girls to eat their evening repast and then settle down for the night as the light slowly faded.

There are few problems that can't be solved with a little thought and research.

Aaaaaaa.....tishoo!

Suddenly the headlines screaming out from everywhere seemed to be about 'Bird Flu,' or avian influenza to give it its full name. Is there anybody in the world who hasn't heard about it? I doubt it, but I suppose there may be a nomadic tribesman living somewhere on the plains of the Serengeti who remains ignorant of this disease – which is probably lucky for him, as according to the doom and gloom merchants it should have killed him by now!

Bird flu had been sporadically rearing its ugly head here and there all over Europe, but the UK had mercifully remained free of it, apart from a dead swan washed ashore in Scotland that had sparked a big scare. No actual cases of H5N1, the deadly strain that can affect humans, had appeared here.

Any Fool Can Be A.......

Suddenly that all changed, and was frighteningly close.

Bird flu was diagnosed as the culprit that had killed a lot of turkeys on a Bernard Matthews' farm in Norfolk. There is an old saying that 'There is no such thing as bad publicity,' meaning that however bad things are, the publicity is still good for your company. Bernard Matthews was about to discover that this was a fallacy as the fallout from the outbreak came close to ruining the company. It turned out that their 'Norfolk Turkeys' were in fact bred in Hungary and then shipped live to the UK. The farm was villified in the media and the public stopped buying their products.

For us the effects were dramatic as we suddenly found ourselves in a 'Restriction Zone' with all the problems that this caused.

Basically the immediate area around the outbreak was declared a 'Protection Zone' where all birds had to be under cover and all poultry within this area were blood tested regularly and any risky contacts meant that the flock affected was destroyed as a precaution. A further ring around this area was a 'Surveillance Zone' where birds had to be kept under cover. Virtually the whole of Suffolk was made a 'Restriction Zone' and owners were urged to keep their birds under cover. No poultry movements at all were allowed in any of the zones, which meant that we couldn't sell any of our spare birds or buy new ones. We also couldn't buy or sell any hatching eggs.

We had bought bird-proof netting and tarpaulins to protect our runs, but as the outbreak hit at a time when we didn't have many birds we decided that we didn't need to go to all that trouble and instead we just kept the birds inside their houses. The sheds were plenty big enough for them to have room enough to live happy lives without the need to use the runs.

To be honest we wondered why we bothered as none of the other chook keepers on the allotments seemed to take a blind bit of notice of the restrictions and all the other birds were still loose in their runs. If there were to be a case of H5N1 on our fields, then our flock would be slaughtered anyway.

There was absolutely no bio security in place and allotment holders wandered freely around the plots visiting friends and reports in the media alleged that French farmers were still-free ranging their flocks inside Protection Zones.

The story ran for weeks and weeks. Bird Flu was going to make the jump to humans and we were all going to die. Well, most of us would. Okay, some of us would. Okay, so it was all a 'Sell more newspapers' plot because nobody in the UK actually died from avian influenza.

It did have one upside for us. The government were (and still are) paranoid about the possibility of bird flu making the transition to humans, as millions died from a mutant form in 1918/9. The danger is that if you are suffering from conventional flu and come into contact with the bird flu virus, then the two bugs may crossbreed and create a superbug. Most of the human deaths from bird flu had been in primitive countries where the chicken keepers virtually ate, slept and sadly died with their stock.

The UK government decided to give free flu vaccinations to poultry keepers who were registered with DEFRA, and Sue and I have had our jabs every year.

We awoke one morning to find a bright yellow leaflet on our doorstep. It was from Suffolk Police and was notifying us that our stolen car had been found. Yeah right. The police had clearly stuck it through the wrong door.

Any Fool Can Be A.......

I wandered into our front room to phone and tell them that they were pillocks and glanced out of the window as I drew back the curtains. Our driveway was empty, apart from some broken glass.

Our car *had* indeed been stolen. I rang the police very politely with no mention of pillocks and they told me that it had been recovered and taken to a garage some miles away. I was not impressed. I was even less impressed when the garage told me that it would be charging me nearly £500 before I could take the car home.

The dilemma was solved when I saw the car – it wouldn't be driving anywhere ever again. My beautiful Saab 9000 had been completely trashed. To rub salt into the wound, the two sacks of chicken feed that had been in it were missing.

There were, however, several tin trays full of some sort of engineer's tools in the back which weren't mine. They were obviously the ill-gotten gains of a burglary somewhere, but the police weren't interested when I rang them.

The car had clearly been in a couple of collisions, and the thieves had even stopped to change one of the front wheels at some time, using the spare.

They must have kerbed it again though, as the other front tyre and the newly fitted spare were both blown. The front suspension was virtually collapsed, and there was bodywork damage everywhere. It had been dumped outside an isolated country house from where they had stolen another car.

So I was now carless and a frustrating battle with the insurers began. It probably wasn't helped by the fact that I hadn't told them I had picked up a couple of speeding convictions, because they set about being as difficult as possible. The whole case was handed over to an independent assessor.

Eventually, having been to inspect the wreck, he opened his phone call with "What a beautiful car," and then offered me £400 as a payment. I agreed that it was a lovely car and told him to come back with an offer of £800 as I couldn't replace it for less. A couple of days later he rang me to say that I was right and that £800 was a fair price. It still took the insurers another month to pay me though. When the renewal came through I immediately changed to another company!

In the meantime I went back to my old friend Ebay. I had decided that a Volvo Estate was the best bet for our new needs, but anything remotely modern would be too much money for me, or was over on the other side of the country.

Suddenly a new listing appeared – a nice car with an immaculate service history, low mileage and nearby. A quick email to the seller got his address and an agreement for me to view and I dragged my son off to take a look at it immediately. After the fastest journey in history we arrived to find that the Volvo was every bit as nice as described, having been owned by a lady who only used it for the school run. Less than eighty five thousand miles on a car over ten years old – for a Volvo that is barely running the engine in! The car was worth £1500 easily and was on at a start price of £800 with no bids. The seller wanted shot of it as soon as possible and my £760 offer was accepted. We brought the car plus a huge wad of service history home in very high spirits.

A hundred quid to fit a tow bar and we would be back in business.

Any Fool Can Be A.......
Okay, we're M.A.D.

By now Sue was becoming a veteran charity shopper and most of my new shirts arrived via this route. Nice shirts that were originally twenty pounds in M&S found their way into my wardrobe for a couple of quid. Work boots and shoes came from Ebay or car boot sales. Trousers were a problem as I'm so tall, but this difficulty was solved by the six quid a pair selection available in supermarkets. I didn't really like what they represent in terms of sweated labour in India or the Far East and transportation right round the world, but an empty wallet overcame my scruples. This sartorial elegance isn't my allotment garb, they are far too good for that. No, my lottie clothes are torn and patched combat trousers in the winter, frayed shorts in the summer and similarly torn and patched shirts. A sweatband made from a torn piece of cotton sheet completes the Rambo ensemble. Is it any wonder that nervous young mums and their children cross the road to avoid me when I return home carrying a heavy bag with stiff chicken legs sticking out of it?

Sue had also discovered the world of Ebay. I think that showing her how to use the computer may have been a mistake. She found that she could get her favourite 'Hotter' brand shoes (retail price £50+) brand new for £5-£10 and so she became the Imelda Marcos of the downshifting world!

Her favourite M&S skirts could also be picked up for as little as 99p.

We needed some extra chairs as there wasn't enough seating available when all our kids descended upon us at once with their other halves. We got round this by buying a mixture of pre-war Lloyd Loom woven chairs in various styles which Sue then painted in a nice matt green colour that matched our carpet. She finished them off by making a matching cushion for each from a big piece of Laura Ashley fabric that she got for one pound from......yes, a charity shop.

I re-covered our net tunnel with yet more of the plastic netting – that huge roll really must rate as the bargain of the century – and added an extension to the side by building a wall from three foot high chicken wire and covering it with yet more of the netting. Being a tall lad I can just about step over it, and only occasionally fall base over apex when doing so. The tunnel and annexe easily cover an area twenty feet by twenty feet, which is ample for growing our cabbages, broccoli and sprouts and protecting them from the voracious local pigeon population.

I had fancied adding nuts to our menu, and so tried planting some Kent cobnut kernels bought from the greengrocer in flowerpots over winter. A surprisingly large percentage of them germinated and I planted the eight young plants along the spare strip of ground beside the net tunnel. As they grow they will help to shield our vegetables from the cutting north wind. As I type this the two year old plants are now three feet tall or so, and I'm hoping that we might get our first crop this year. They won't be Kent cobs of course as I think these are grafted onto rootstock and so nuts won't grow true, but we should get hazel nuts. Assuming that the squirrels don't get them first that is......

Rosie also came into season. I realised this the moment that I arrived at the allotment gates early one morning.

I think that most of the people on the surrounding housing estate also realised that something pretty unusual was happening. She was standing on top of her heap of pallets and bellowing the news to the rest of the world. This was followed by a short pause as she sniffed the air speculatively and peered all around the allotments hopefully. She would then pump her lungs up enthusiastically and bellow again.

Any Fool Can Be A.......

This lasted for forty eight hours. Basically she was screaming, "Hey big boy, here I am – come and get me!"

But of course there was no big boy to hear her calls, or if there was he was playing hard to get. She bellowed so loud that perhaps the wild goats on the Orme peninsula in Wales heard her, but since the police warned motorists not to pick up hitchhiking goats on the M4 it has been very difficult for them to travel around. Gertie came into season just a week after Rosie.

We stepped up our attempts to find a billy, but with no success. We discovered that goats can carry a sexually transmitted disease known as CAE, and that anybody who had a billy would demand that they see a current vet's certificate showing that our girls had a clean bill of health before they would let their lad anywhere near them. All the reputable herds are CAE tested every year.

We had no option but to cough up for a vet to visit and take blood samples, and for them to be laboratory tested. I don't think the vet had done this with goats before as she had difficulty finding the jugular, and when she finally did manage it there was blood spraying out everywhere. This was rather scary to watch and probably even more scary if you were the goat, but the results were clear, although my threadbare wallet took another big hit.

The good part was that the vet complimented us on the health and wellbeing of the goats, and she said that they were both a lovely size, neither too fat nor too thin. She also said that our housing was much better than many that she had seen and that their pen was a good size.

We felt totally vindicated. The show goat fraternity could stick their opinions where the sun didn't shine - our goats were thriving in the 'totally unsuitable' accommodation in which we were housing them.

With no success in our search for a billy we decided to contact the rare breeds farm to which Julie's billy Peter had been sold. So one day we set out, paid our entrance fees and had a walk round Baylham Rare Breeds Farm. This name may ring a bell with some of you. If it does, you will know where this story is eventually headed.

We discovered that Baylham is a family run farm and everybody mucks in with all the jobs, and it was the son Neil who was on duty at the entrance gate. Although the family are members of the Suffolk Smallholders' Society I had never met them before, and I had grave doubts that they would be interested in the sorry plight of a couple of M.A.D. people and their goats.

I couldn't have been more wrong. My nervous enquiry about their billy was met with enthusiasm and the promise of help. They turned out to be really lovely people who cared deeply about their animals. They were quite willing to take our girls in for a week towards the end of the year, once we had established their season patterns and as long as it fitted into their own schedules for moving animals on and off the farm. Bringing our goats in would force them into a shutdown for a week, with no animal movements allowed. A large working farm has to get their timings just right.

We had a pleasant hour or two wandering around their vast holding, admiring the many rare animals. A big fat Kune Kune sow with her huge litter of delightful little piglets made me particularly jealous. As we reluctantly made our way back to the entrance we bumped into Neil again and stood for a while chatting about his farm, and what we were trying to achieve. We were interrupted by his wife who came to tell Neil that one of their Golden Guernseys was in labour and having difficulties. We thanked Neil for his promise of help and prepared to leave so that he could get on with his urgent duties, but he insisted that we should come with him to see the birth.

As we neared the field where the goats were housed we could hear an animal screaming in pain. Goats have a very low pain tolerance threshold and will in fact just give up and lay down to die. Geraldine was obviously not enjoying her kidding. We followed Neil into the paddock and over to the field shelter where all the racket was coming from, trying to ignore the curious looks from the visitors to the farm who were lined up along the rails, morbidly trying to locate the source of the agonised screams. Goat kiddings obviously have something in common with road traffic accidents – passers by just *have* to stop and stare.

When we looked inside the field shelter the first thing we saw was a lovely long haired blonde Golden Guernsey resting placidly, with an absolutely *gorgeous* young kid beside her. Neil told us that the kid was born a week ago, and he was disappointed that it was a billy.

Fresh bellowing drew our attention sharply to the other side of the shelter where a clearly distressed Geraldine was panting and screaming and clearly having contractions. Neil quickly examined her and showed us what the problem was – the kid was positioned wrongly. When the goat kid starts to put in an appearance the first thing that you see in a normal birth is the tips of both front hooves and a nose. Geraldine's kid was showing one hoof and an ear, so a leg was tucked back and the head twisted. This would make it a difficult birth and possibly a fatal one for the kid.

Neil dealt with the situation calmly and quickly, inserting his hand into Geraldine's nether regions and locating the other foreleg before gently bringing it forward, then carefully turning the kid so that the head was positioned correctly. Another scream from Geraldine and it was all over, with a soggy heap of kid lying bleating in the straw. A quick examination showed that the kid was another male, much to Neil's frustration. Neil placed the kid by Geraldine's head and the proud mum gave her youngster a good licking whilst we oohed and aahed with pleasure.

A few minutes later she started more contractions and very quickly delivered another kid normally; unbelievably, it was yet another male.

Neil just shook his head stoically. We wondered what we were letting ourselves in for, but we had no idea that being present at that birth would prove to be such a valuable experience for us later.

Dark clouds move in

We were already in the bird flu protection zone when a new threat suddenly appeared.

Foot and Mouth disease was discovered in Surrey, in fields right next to the government disease research laboratories in Pirbright. The media immediately leapt upon this strange coincidence and their allegations proved to be completely true, something that must be a world first! It transpired that FMD had in fact escaped from the laboratories through a broken drain, leaked into the field and promptly rampaged all over Surrey.

Now bearing in mind that our girls had come from Surrey, this wasn't the best news for us to hear.

Add to this that an FMD control zone was put into place, and suddenly our matrimonial arrangements for the girls were looking very precarious.

Any Fool Can Be A.......

Baylham farm has thousands of visitors every year and suddenly those thousands of visitors became a very real threat to the health and wellbeing of all the animals kept there. The FMD virus is particularly strong, and can live for long periods away from its host. That seemingly innocuous layer of mud on your wellies where you visited Farmer Giles last week can suddenly become a hotbed of disease as you walk through some other farmer's fields or cow sheds.

Animal movements across the whole of the UK were halted, so despite the fact that we were a hundred miles away from the outbreaks, this meant that we couldn't move *Gertie* and *Rosie* the five miles to see Peter. Even if we had been able to move them I don't think that Peter's owners would have been pleased to see them at that time. Suddenly things were looking very dangerous, with both bird flu and foot and mouth seemingly loitering on every corner.

The media went into a frenzy and much worse was soon to come. Responsible journalism seems to have gone out of the window in recent years and it is now all about hype and sensationalism. Instead of reporting the facts calmly and reassuringly, the press strive to drive the population into a blind panic. Who remembers Sars in 2003? It was going to kill us all, according to the media. I doubt that the average man in the street could even tell you anything about it now.

The source of the FMD infection was very quickly traced to the broken drain in the research laboratories, and although there were several new outbreaks up to ten miles away due to human or animal movements, the virus didn't extend beyond the Surrey boundaries. It wasn't too long before the movement restrictions in the rest of the country were lifted and we could breathe again.

Meanwhile, back at Goat Central the newcomers to the allotments had been attracting a lot of attention. Allotment holders brought their grandchildren over to see them. At a time when bio-security and isolation were at the forefront of our minds, we were having to cope with hordes of people trekking through our plots.

We discovered that the schoolkids on the next plot had enjoyed a day out, having a nice barbecue on their allotment. Fine so far. We also heard that they had been feeding the unwanted undercooked or burnt bits to our chickens! This was a recipe for disaster. Something had to be done, but what?

Then one Saturday I sat at home in the early afternoon feeling most distressed, and I couldn't think why. I kept getting the urge to go to the allotments, but I had been over in the morning and fed the goats and chickens, and had other things to get on with at home. I wasn't due to go back over to the fields until it was time for the goats' evening feed. But that nagging feeling wouldn't go away and in the end I decided to pop over and take a look to satisfy myself that all was well.

I arrived at the allotments to find the gates wide open. This was nothing unusual, especially on a Saturday, as they would often be opened for deliveries and Saturday was the favourite muck-delivery day.

However what I could see in the distance *wasn't* so good. Two large brown dogs were being chased around the fields by irate plotholders.

But hold on a minute........dogs don't have things sticking out of the tops of their heads. The girls had somehow gotten loose or somebody must have let them out!

I hurriedly closed and locked the gates. Any deliveries could wait – if the goats got onto the road it didn't bear thinking about.

Any Fool Can Be A......

I dashed over to where *Gertie* and *Rosie* were leading their followers a merry dance, getting ahead of them and then stopping for a leisurely meal from a tasty looking cabbage or sweetcorn plant on somebody's plot. This would sometimes lead to an angry shout and another person joining the group of chasers.

I arrived on the scene puffing and blowing and the posse backed off to leave me to get on with the recapturing of my two escapees. This soon proved to be easier said than done as the girls were now very agitated, having been chased hither and thither, and they had discovered that the outside world was actually a giant walk-in pantry. They weren't about to be led placidly back to their pen.

My efforts proved to be just as futile as those of the allotment posse, as the girls danced around keeping just ahead of my attempts to catch them. The big difference was that they now had an audience – an audience that was taking great pleasure in watching me dive around and was now waiting for me to fall flat on my backside. I knew that I had to catch *Gertie* as if I managed that, then *Rosie* would follow along behind her mum. The longer they were loose, the more risk there was that they would do some serious damage somewhere, and their future on the allotments would be in danger. It would only take one complaint and the council would withdraw our permission to keep them.

In desperation I went to the hedgerow surrounding the fields and broke off a large hazel branch from a big bush. I knew that as browsers goats preferred trees and bushes on their menu in preference to just about anything, and that the woody twigs would be devoured greedily.

I waved the branch in *Gertie's* direction. She gazed at it with interest, but then looked suspiciously at me. She took a tentative step forward, staring at me as she did so, and then another step. Suddenly a member of the amused audience dashed up from behind her and tried to grab her. Both goats took to their heels and dashed away while I was left berating the failed capturer (kidnapper?) angrily, questioning his parenthood and the dubious working capability of his single brain cell.

I walked slowly towards *Gertie* again, talking to her gently and reassuringly, all the time holding out and offering her the hazel branch. She didn't come towards me but she didn't shy off and run either. I wafted the branch in front of her and saw her nostrils twitch. *Rosie* meanwhile was munching away contentedly on somebody's beetroot patch – if mum wasn't worried then neither was she.

Gertie took a nibble from a leaf on the hazel branch and decided that it was acceptable. She set to with a vengeance and I slowly edged round to one side of her.

I gently tickled her back and when this got no reaction I gradually inched my hand forward, stroking as I went. *Gertie* was now only interested in the hazel twigs and was ignoring me. I fondled her ears, took a deep breath......and grabbed a horn. Thank God that I had insisted on goats with handlebars!

She bucked and reared but realised that her allotment jaunt was over and I led her back to her pen followed meekly by young *Rosie*. When I got there I found the gate standing open and the padlock hanging from the mesh where I had left it. I had shut them in after feeding them, but had forgotten to lock the door and the wind had blown it open.

I walked home in a daze thinking of what might have happened if they had gotten out onto the busy road.

A couple of days of pondering and I had the answer. I started fencing off my top two plots with old rolls of chainlink that I had picked up here and there. The first side to be barricaded off was the one between my plots and the school patch, and then I gradually worked my way round the perimeter.

When I had finished the goats couldn't get very far even if they managed to slip past me, and only my own fruit and vegetables would be in danger, and the fencing stopped the locals from making their trips in to see Mike's menagerie.

It also protected my patch of giant pumpkins from being raided, as I had noticed people eyeing them up. Most allotment folk are honest, friendly and helpful, but there are a few that find it easier to take the fruits of other people's labour rather than do the labour themselves. We had lost butternut squashes in the past and our neighbour had his whole apple crop taken. We even had somebody help themselves to our rhubarb, when we would have given it freely if asked.

So our barricade proved itself to be useful in more ways than one and despite several more escapes (I never did find the shovel that they used to dig the tunnel), the goats never again got onto other plots, although they did strip the fruit off one of my apple trees.

Gertie and Rosie go on holiday

Sounds like the title of an Enid Blyton 'Famous Five' book, doesn't it?

Really it should be 'Gertie and Rosie Find Sex in the Country,' which is probably more Jackie Collins than Enid Blyton.

Not only did the goats get a holiday – they got two, and we

managed to sneak a short break in as well.

We knew that we wouldn't be able to have a holiday once the goats were milking, so we had arranged to stay with a friend in Yorkshire for a few days if the movement restrictions were ever lifted and *Gertie* and *Rosie* got the chance to enjoy Peter's attentions in Baylham. Sod's Law stepped in, because when we rang our friend in Yorkshire and said "we can come next week," it turned out that she would be away herself. We were so disappointed, but then we rang somebody on the ACL forum who advertised holiday accommodation for livestock and they agreed to take our goats for a week. They had goats themselves and so we were happy that they could look after ours properly.

Our GGs would be taken straight from Baylham to their B&B and get to meet some Anglo-Nubian distant relations, plus pigs, turkeys, ducks and chickens.

The great day arrived and as I approached their pen I could hear a goat bleating away at the top of its lungs – *Rosie* had come into season a day early. Both the goats were loaded into the trailer, and we took bags of their food with us so that they wouldn't get stomach upsets from eating unfamiliar food.

After an uneventful short trip we arrived at Baylham and were told to release our goats into the paddock where we had witnessed the kidding a few months before. *Gertie* started to investigate the field shelter and check to see if it was edible with *Rosie* trotting around beside her, but then there was an unmistakable smell carried on the wind and Peter appeared, being led by one of the workers. When he was released there was no mistaking the leer on his face as he galloped full pelt across the field towards the girls. *Gertie* had at first started walking towards him, but when it was clear that his intentions were amorous she turned and legged it in the opposite direction, followed by *Rosie*. Peter was ready for this though and neatly maneuvered himself between them and headed *Rosie* off. It was all over in the blink of an eye. Evidently goats, like chickens, have no idea of foreplay. We did wonder if Peter suffered from premature ejaculation, but it seems this is normal.

He turned towards *Gertie* expectantly but she was clearly unimpressed with his performance and butted him away. He wandered over to Sue for a piece of bread instead. Such is the lot of males the world over. Maybe this is why there is an obesity problem.

We shared all our goodies out between the three goats and headed off home feeling not unlike pimps.

Neil had agreed that we could come to see our goats as often as we liked, so we turned up early the next morning armed with plenty of titbits but the paddock was empty.......and so was the field shelter.

We wondered what had happened to the goats and set off to investigate.

A familiar aroma wafted on the breeze and I followed my nose. We turned into the farmyard and there, in one of the covered pens, were the three absentees with the two females looking like butter wouldn't melt in their mouths and one male looking hopefully for food. Peter had evidently decided that Christmas had come early with unlimited sex and lots of feasting on the agenda.

A farmhand appeared and explained that two very bad girls had kept jumping the wire fence at the back of the paddock and disappearing into the surrounding countryside looking for tasty morsels. Poor Peter was left in the paddock to carry the can. In the end they had no option but to pen all three goats.

Gertie and *Rosie* had lost their chance to have a week's holiday in a nice big paddock, and instead were in a pen smaller than their one at home, shut in with a billy on hormone overdrive.

We visited them each day and on the fourth day Peter was in a very agitated mood. When I entered the pen and approached *Gertie* he swung one of his huge horns in my direction, so I scarpered quickly. He started charging the steel pen and butting the gate before rubbing himself against *Gertie*, who promptly butted him meaningfully. It looked like *Gertie* was coming into season and Peter could sense it, but she wasn't ready for canoodling yet. Poor Peter was simply a very frustrated lad.

The next day all was peaceful again. *Gertie* stank and Peter was only interested in food, so we guessed that the wedding nuptials had taken place.

The following day we turned up with our trailer and loaded two very smelly girls up ready to take them on the second week of their holiday.

When we arrived at the smallholding hotel we were greeted by two very curious Anglo-Nubian goats hanging over the rail of their stall, looking for all the world like a pair of boisterous freshly-shorn Old English Sheepdogs. They really were a comical pair, looking for fuss and food in equal measure. What am I talking about? They were *goats* – theyjust wanted food!

Gertie and *Rosie* were led into the next stall and *Gertie* instantly started attacking her neighbours through a three inch gap in the planking. She obviously didn't think that a holiday should be any different to any other day.

We were wandering round the smallholding and admiring the pigs, turkeys and chickens when suddenly *Gertie* was there beside us. She had worked a neat escape trick, climbing out through the hole designed to let her feed from her manger. The hole was quickly boarded up and the girls were fed from buckets for the rest of the week.

We escaped to Yorkshire for three days. We had a pleasant break helping our friend to drink her sloe gin. The things you have to force yourself to do to keep other people happy.

We all went for a ramble up on the moors, starting from the village of Goathland where the TV programme 'Heartbeat' is filmed. The local hunt was assembled in the car park and set off with horns blowing as we trudged off into the hills.

Steady rain turned to sleet. As we sat miserably beneath a large tree eating our soggy sandwiches we heard a steam train approaching along the track below us. I grabbed my camera and snapped a fantastic photograph of *Sir Nigel Gresley* as she thundered through. A sister to the famous *Mallard*, it was exciting to see her.

As we finished our lunch the sleet turned to snow – quite heavy snow, in fact – and we cut short our hike and headed back down into the valley, the landscape now turning white around us. We drove down off the moors on white roads, in a winter wonderland. We heard on the radio the next morning that the hill roads were now blocked. It was only the end of November.

We had also looked at one or two houses whilst we were up in Yorkshire as land is cheaper there and we hankered after our own smallholding, but we decided that the weather was trying to tell us something. We returned to a much milder East Anglia having enjoyed an eventful three days. As we left our friend's village a barn owl flew along beside us for at least a hundred yards and I tried very hard not to drive into a ditch as I admired it.

Despite the long drive home we were up early the next morning to go and collect the girls. They had finally learned how to behave themselves as there were no black marks in their report. And so, with a pair of excited Anglo-Nubians hanging over the fence watching, we led the girls back to the trailer and took them home.

As we settled them back into their pen, tickled their ears and fed them goodies, we pondered just how many goats there might now be in our care.

Radio stars

*G*ertie and *Rosie* suddenly found themselves in the limelight a few weeks after their visit to Baylham.

I was listening to BBC Radio Suffolk early one morning when I heard the DJ Mark Murphy talking about chicken welfare. Hugh Fearnley-Whittingstall's programme 'Hugh's Chicken Run' had been aired on TV the night before and had become a hot topic in the media.

For those of you who didn't see the series HFW is a campaigner against battery-raised egg and meat birds. He maintains that poultry can be raised in much better conditions for a reasonable cost if the demand is there, so his programmes are aimed at educating the great British public to eat free range or at least barn reared poultry. It is a campaign that is close to our hearts as it epitomises all our own reasons for going M.A.D.

Mark was asking listeners what type of poultry they bought and I emailed him to say that I ate my own chickens, raised my own fruit and veg and kept goats, all on council allotments. If I could do it, so could anybody.

There followed a flurry of emails exchanged between myself and BBC researchers and before we knew it Mark was coming to see *Gertie* and *Rosie* the next day.

Mark turned out to be a really nice chap, very friendly and easy to talk to. A local boy made good, he is very much part of the community, having a seat at Ipswich Town FC in the North Stand with the lads, and taking part in and promoting all sorts of local events. He chatted to us in our lounge to help us relax and then headed off to the allotments with us. I was very much at my ease, having been on the radio and in the newspapers before and speaking regularly in public, but Sue was a bundle of nerves as she is basically rather shy.

Mark walked us through a rehearsal on the allotments, asking us the questions that he would ask on the way round, and then we did it for real.

We ended up in the goat pen where our two legged eating machines tested everything for edibility, including Mark's coat and wedding ring. Luckily he kept his microphone out of reach. Mark posed with me for a picture for our website, and as he headed off back to the studio we gave him a box of our eggs.

The next day we waited with bated breath as the programme began, and every now and then they plugged the upcoming interview with "Mike and his goats."

When it was finally aired we were thrilled with the result. We were even more amused that after the interview the presenters proceeded to cook (and enjoy) our eggs on the air! Amidst all the banter and jokes we felt that a few more people had heard the word about animal welfare and healthy eating. Maybe one or two more shoppers would now buy free range instead of intensively reared chickens.

Gertie and *Rosie* were totally unimpressed by their stardom as Mark hadn't brought them any titbits - the only thing that interested them. *Gertie* did stand by her gate the next day with a pen tucked behind her ear ready to satisfy any requests for autographs, but when the fan club didn't appear she quietly considered eating the pen instead.

Meanwhile they were both growing. *Gertie* was getting particularly big, and we worried about how many kids she might be carrying. I began to have nightmares about the birth, and an ominous sense of impending doom settled on me.

Everybody 'goaty' told us that there was nothing to worry about as the goats did all the hard work and it always all turned out fine. I recalled *Geraldine's* difficult kidding at Baylham and I wasn't convinced.

We experienced an unusually hot and dry early spring, with high temperatures in March and April and very little rainfall. I was reluctant to start hand watering crops as once you start it you have to keep it up, but many of our vegetables were clearly suffering and so I got the hoses out.

Our autumn planted Japanese onion sets bolted to seed and stayed very small, and although we had sown large numbers of early peas under netting, very few actually germinated. We suspected mice were the culprits.

The credit crunch was beginning to bite for us. Although we have no mortgage we still need an income to pay all the utility bills, run a car and buy the things that we can't live without. Animal feed bills started to rise sharply and fuel costs went through the roof. The need to earn a crust was putting pressure on our already precious time and the weeds on the allotments were receiving less attention.

Our finances suddenly received a boost when our editor friend contacted us – he had started editing a new magazine, *Home Farmer,* and would like us to write for him. This was great news for us as we were really struggling. Shortly after this another magazine got in touch and some more regular writing resulted.

Suddenly we were writing for two magazines every month, and for a third one occasionally. It meant that the weeds grew a bit more on the fields, but at least we could afford to buy chook food.

We had a little bit of excitement one day when we had to call the fire brigade. Our niece Joanne was over from New Zealand at the time and was helping me out with photographs on the allotments. We wanted a shot of the goats and me for *Home Farmer* and Sue had taken fifty or more the day before, with none of them being suitable. One or other of the goats was always wrongly positioned or pulling a silly face, or pointing its bum at the camera – and when they were posed beautifully I would have my eyes closed or not be smiling, or picking my nose or something. It's very hard to get animals to pose, and chickens are even worse! Goats can at least be tempted with food at the right level, but throw corn down for the chooks and they instantly go head down with their bums in the air.

Joanne had taken around a hundred shots and we thought that one of them would be good (yes really, only one) so we were heading home to load them onto the computer to take a better look when we spotted smoke pouring across the field. It was coming from a greenhouse that had its glass totally blacked out by soot. There was a dull red glow inside and the glass panes at one end had shattered, hence the pall of drifting smoke. I ventured closer and realised that the wooden staging inside was on fire, and it had clearly been started by a blackened paraffin heater standing on the staging. Fearing an explosion I withdrew and called 999.

When the fire engine turned up my niece was beside herself with excitement – not on account of the fire, but because of the close proximity of the big hunky firemen! The fire was dealt with quickly and they confirmed that the heater had caught light and set the wooden staging ablaze. The owner would have a lovely job cleaning up afterwards.

This interesting day was eclipsed, however, by monumental events a few days later. I was approached and asked if I would be interested in writing a book!

The publishers of *Home Farmer* also produced a wide variety of books on smallholding related subjects and wanted a poultry book to fit into their range.

My first reaction was that I couldn't do it as I didn't know enough.

Then I thought about it and realised that they weren't looking for a specialist poultry encyclopaedia but a smallholder's handbook – *that* I could do with no problem! Of course it meant a lot more work, and work that I wouldn't get paid for immediately, but I have always loved writing and so couldn't say no. If you will pardon the poor pun, a whole new chapter in our lives was opening up.

Any Fool Can Be A.......
The patter of tiny feet

Both the girls continued to grow, and ate both anything and everything which probably doesn't surprise you as I have already described them as four legged eating machines, but when they are pregnant goats can be very perverse. They will often stop eating for no apparent reason, or become very choosy about what they eat. Thankfully we didn't have this problem. The polytunnel provided lots of early spring greenery for them as our cauliflowers did tremendously well, and we were able to feed them outside leaves on a regular basis to top up any shortfalls and provide a balanced diet.

Unseasonably early warm weather meant that the wild brambles around the field sprouted lovely fresh green leaves very early, and I cut great armfuls of them, tied them in bunches and hung them in the girls' run. It fascinates me how goats can pick all round the thorns with their tongues, stripping the leaves off without damaging themselves on the barbs. They then start from the tips and munch their way down the whole stem, thorns and all.

We were less easy to feed. We barely survived the 'hunger gap' as we ran out of stored onions, carrots and potatoes. Yet again the carrot fly had ruined our carrot crop, despite the fact that we put a two foot high fine mesh netting fence up around them as a barrier. We must have had the only pole-vaulting carrot fly in the UK! A long wet summer had ruined our onions, rotting many of them, whilst a bone dry spring seemed to set the potatoes back badly and we had a poor crop. They were planted in a pretty poor patch of soil though, so we prepared the potato patch with plenty of chicken manure and leaf mould dug in for the following year. At least the early potatoes in the polytunnel saved the day, and broccoli solved the severe greens shortage. We had to buy carrots and onions, sneaking them into our shopping basket when nobody was looking. We couldn't be seen to be *buying* vegetables. We had a reputation to protect!

My sense of impending doom grew with the goats' stomachs. Poor *Gertie* was getting so big she would soon have trouble getting through the doorway to her shed. Both girls had huge udders, and they had to walk in a very bow-legged fashion to avoid falling over them.

Three days before *Rosie* was due to kid I went over to the allotments to feed all the livestock, and when I opened the goats' shed I discovered a dead newbornkid lying just inside the door. Poor *Rosie* had kidded overnight all alone and had lost her baby. She hadn't been particularly big and had now lost what bulk she did have. She was lying quietly in the straw and didn't make a fuss as I entered the shed. She seemed perfectly OK, although subdued. I felt so sad for her.

So five months of pregnancy had come to this; a dead kid. As I squatted down beside to check her over and comfort her I heard a little squeak behind her. *Gertie* was over at the other side of the shed and hungrier than ever, so unless she had learned ventriloquism the noise hadn't come from her.

I edged my way round *Rosie* and checked behind her. Protected by her body and tucked into the corner of the shed were two gorgeous little billy kids! They were perfect in every way except for their sex, but were quite small and weak.

They couldn't get the hang of suckling and it was crucial that they drank very soon. I removed the dead kid, then dashed home and picked ud up a lambing bottle and teat that my friend Jill had sent me, plus a jug, some flannels and some warm water.

Rosie's udders and rear end had to be well washed down as there was blood everywhere from the birth, so I tethered her in a corner of the shed and sorted out her morning feed. She munched away contentedly enough and didn't take a blind bit of notice of what I was doing to her nether regions. Her teats were huge and swollen and I took one tentatively in my hand and squeezed. Bright yellow milk spurted out instantly. I manoeuvred the jug between her legs, and began pumping away nervously, all the time expecting a hoof to fly out in my direction. *Rosie* was as good as gold and totally ignored my clumsy efforts. I quickly filled the jug and emptied it into the bottle before milking some more and refilling it.

It is absolutely essential that newborn kids get a bellyful of the first milk as soon as possible. This milk is full of a substance called colostrum, which is vital to the kid's wellbeing. The colostrum kick starts the kid's rumen, its digestive system, and also carries the mother's antibodies over to the kid to protect it from disease.

Bottle feeding the twins was a grand old game. I think I ended up wearing more milk than the kids actually drank that morning. I milked a further jug from Rosie when I had fed them though, and carefully carried it home. We froze it so that we had something to offer *Gertie's* offspring, should there be a problem with her milk.

There was nothing visibly wrong with the dead kid, which turned out to be another billy. We simply assumed that he was just too weak and that nature had taken its course.

I milked *Rosie* again in the evening and this time managed to get much more into the kids via the bottle. They were both a lot stronger and were beginning to take an interest in Rosie's teats, although they were still unable to get any milk. By the next morning the improvement was remarkable, and although I fed them both to be certain that they had had their fill, I could see that they were both suckling well from *Rosie*.

Gertie wasn't prepared to let the kids near her, but otherwise wasn't really interested in *Rosie* or her kids. To be on the safe side we moved *Rosie* and the boys out of her pen, though. The run next door had a 6′ x 4′ shed used as a chicken coop and the chickens were summarily evicted. I removed the perches and cleaned the shed out thoroughly before laying a deep litter of straw. Our new family took to it instantly and the two kids adopted a nestbox each as their beds. They looked really sweet curled up inside them.

Meanwhile I eyed up *Gertie* nervously. She was huge. *Rosie* had been slim and had produced three kids – how many was *Gertie* carrying?

Whilst our friends had been right about *Rosie* producing her offspring naturally and without help, this didn't fill me with confidence for *Gertie* and my nagging fears didn't go away.

Once the kids were feeding properly I didn't milk *Rosie* any more. I decided to let the kids get the full benefit of the milk and I could wait until after *Gertie's* kidding before starting regular milking.

Just the thought of it

Having produced two billy kids I now faced a somewhat distasteful job. I've already mentioned how badly billies smell, especially in the breeding season. They acquire this smell at around three months old and incredibly, even at this age, they are sexually mature and will try to mate with their mother/sister/cousin or probably even the dog if it stays still long enough!

We knew that castration solves this problem and would also ensure a heavier carcass when it is time for the deadly deed to be done. It also gave us the option that if we were unable to bring ourselves to slaughter them, then we could sell them as pets. We were not keen on this idea though because most people have the misconception that goats are great lawnmowers, and they are very misunderstood creatures. They are herd animals and are not happy kept on their own. They are actually browsers, not grazers, so grass doesn't interest them unless it is very long. We had always been highly critical of chicken keepers who hatch eggs without giving any forethought to what they will do with hatched cockerels, so unless we were to become hypocrites, we knew that we had to plan ahead and face these difficult decisions. We knew that the billies would have to have the chop in more ways than one.

As soon as she heard that we had billies our friend Jill posted us a tool similar to a pair of pliers and some small rubber rings. You pop a rubber ring over the prongs at the end of the tool and then grip the handles, which expands the ring. You then have to manoeuvre the ring over the young goat's testes and release it. The ring simply contracts, the blood supply is cut off and the testes then shrivel up and drop off.

It sounds easy, doesn't it?

All male readers of this book are probably now clenching their knees firmly together and wincing. Just the thought of it brings tears to my eyes, I know.

But it had to be done, so Sue and I set off to the fields armed with a couple of the rubber rings. The job must be done within the first few days of a billy's life or their bits grow too big and the ring won't fit over them – it then becomes a job for the vet with a scalpel and a general anaesthetic.

As we entered the pen both kids ran over to us for some attention, which made the job even harder. We had decided that we mustn't get too friendly with them as we faced the possibility of taking them to slaughter in a few months, but it was very difficult.

I grabbed one of the kids, and passed him to Sue for her to hold in position so that I could get at his personal bits. It is a tricky job as you have to make sure that both testes are firmly within the ring, but that you don't trap anything else close by, such as nipples. I managed to get the ring in place and released it. He gave a bit of a squeak. I examined my handiwork – it was probably a little tight, but it was on properly. Sue let him go and he dashed across to the corner of the pen. No, that's not true. He kind of did a cross between a waddle and a hop across the pen, where he stood and glared at us defiantly. His brother meantime had seen what had happened and was standing in the opposite corner glaring at us, equally defiant. I kind of sensed that we had overcome the problem of getting too close to them – they weren't about to let us get anywhere near them again!

Catching the second kid proved to be fun and we chased him round the pen until we cornered him. He was very quickly dealt with and I managed to get the ring a little further on for him, so there was less pressure on his testicles. I felt sorry for the first one as his undoubtedly hurt a bit more, but there was no chance of a 'second go' – once these rings are on, they are on.

Both kids curled up together in a corner of their shed and whimpered a bit to each other in sympathy. The next day they appeared to have virtually forgotten about it – although they gave me a wide birth. A week later their testes were black and shrivelled, and a couple of weeks later there was absolutely no sign of them.

A lot was going to happen in those weeks though……..

Any Fool Can Be A.......

Up to my armpits in it

The following Saturday I was on the allotments at 8.00am to feed and water all the livestock. *Gertie* was very vocal, making some pretty strange noises. She either had a bellyache or something was happening in the kidding department, and my guess was that she was ready.

She continued to call after being let out into her run and at 10.00am her waters broke as she was clambering around on her adventure playground. She carried on as if nothing had happened and ate and drank normally until 2.00pm, when she very suddenly went into labour and very quickly produced a small dead kid – again a billy – that hadn't formed correctly and had its eyelids sealed shut and a sizeable hole at its navel.

We were deeply shocked by this, but worse was to come.

Gertie had strong contractions for about an hour and then they stopped, at which pouint she stood up and walked about, accepted some cabbage leaves that I offered her and ate hay and carried on as though she didn't have a care in the world. We began to wonder if it was all over, despite her large size. We tried calling the vet from my mobile phone, but on a Saturday afternoon we just got an answering service. Sue went home and brought back sandwiches and a flask of tea and just as we started on them *Gertie* again went into labour, but this time it was accompanied by screams of pain. An examination revealed a head emerging, but no front hooves as is usual. I knew from our witnessing the kidding on Baylham Farm that I had to get the kid into the delivery position, but with my large hands in such a small space I struggled to find the front legs, which were obviously tucked back and jammed. Sue had a try, managed to find a hoof and brought it forward....but it turned out to be a tiny, very dead *hind* leg!

We knew that we were in serious trouble. We were now facing the prospect of losing not only the kids but *Gertie* too, as she had a very large and live kid with its front legs tucked back, but jammed side by side with a dead one in the breech position. The kids eyes were open and looking at me beseechingly, and it was breathing with difficulty. We tried frantically to reach the vet as we were still waiting for a call back from the messaging service, but it was becoming clear that we would have to do something ourselves. Although terrified, and with *Gertie* screaming continuously, I somehow managed to ease the dead kid back in a little to allow enough room to gently turn the live kid slightly so that I could find a front leg. I couldn't find the other one, but *Gertie* was pushing strenuously now and my very slight repositioning of the two emerging kids seemed to have cleared the birth canal slightly. With a little help from me the live kid was delivered safely, leaving a dead rear leg hanging from poor *Gertie's* rear end. The body came free quite easily and turned out to be a very small foetus with no eyes. It had obviously been dead for some weeks as it was nothing more than skin and bones. Unbelievably, all three kids were billies!

The vet finally rang us and ran through what we had done, and congratulated us on managing so well. She instructed me to do a full internal examination to check that there were no other kids present, which was not the most pleasant task I have ever carried out! Sue held my mobile phone to my ear with one hand and hung onto *Gertie* with the other. The birth passage was already beginning to close, and as I inserted my muscular arm *Gertie* winced a bit, but was otherwise very good. Up to my armpit in goat, I hung onto her legs with my free hand and felt around inside her. There were two very strange big airbags floating around inside, but no more kids. The vet explained that these were bags of fluid and that in a normal birth one of these would be pushed out before each kid, and would be burst by the contractions. This was the breaking of the waters that would lubricate the birth canal in a more normal birth. So poor old *Gertie* had been trying to give birth to two kids at once through a dry canal. I gingerly removed my blood covered arm, much to *Gertie's* relief.

As *Gertie* was now up and licking the youngster, and he was trying to find her udders, the vet didn't feel it was necessary for us to have an expensive weekend callout, and arranged for me to pick up some antibiotics from the surgery on Sunday morning. While we were discussing these arrangements *Gertie* had more contractions and there was suddenly a lot of afterbirth hanging free, but the vet assured us this was normal.

The surviving kid was enormous, and bigger than either of *Rosie's* kids which were now a week old. It was clear that the other two kids had died early on in the pregnancy and that he had gotten all the nourishment. He kept trying to find a teat to feed from, but *Gertie* had an enormous and pendulous udder and her teats were very low. He was searching too high to be able to find them, so we bottle fed him to be on the safe side.

At 8.00pm we finally and reluctantly left as dusk settled over the allotments. It had been a very long day.

Fortunately there was no passing police patrol as we walked home together, with me looking like a mad axeman covered in blood and a shell-shocked Sue doing a passable impression of my next victim!

Sue said very firmly, "Well, we're not going through all *that* again!"

When we got back home I proudly emailed the Golden Guernsey group telling them of our exploits and how we had managed to cope with the difficult kidding. Within a couple of hours there was a really nasty reply from somebody who claimed that we should have left *Gertie* alone, that we shouldn't have interfered with the birth, and that we may well have introduced bacteria internally and may well have killed her. This message came from somebody who was involved in the running of a big city farm, and its effect was devastating on us. We were mortified as we thought we had done so well. The fact that the vet had told us we had done well carried no weight with this woman, who was scathing in her attacks.

All the senior goat keepers on the list very quickly jumped to our defence, and the woman eventually resigned from the group. As far as we were concerned we were exonerated, but the whole episode left a really bad taste in our mouths.

The goat group had been a huge source of help for us, with any questions answered quickly, but now we felt that we couldn't post news items for fear of being attacked again. We were soon going to need advice on slaughtering the billies too and I sensed that this issue could cause fresh arguments. Luckily we still had Jill, our friendly goat lady, and we could ring her up at any time we were unsure of something.

The following day we collected the penicillin from the surgery and I gave Gertie her shot. By now I was highly experienced in giving injections.

The vet called in to see both the girls on Monday morning and pronounced herself very pleased with their condition, so we breathed a sigh of relief. I asked the vet whether we had done the right thing in assisting with the kidding and she assured us that we had, pointing out the size of the kid that had survived. She stressed that with a dead kid jammed beside it, and a dry birth as well, the outcome was not likely to be a good one.

We had been called Tom and Barbara for some time because of

our *Good Life* aspirations, but now some people started calling me James Herriot!

Trouble and Strife

Of course, whilst all this was going on with the goats I wasn't just sitting around on my bum waiting for the births. It was early spring and there was lots of weeding, hoeing and digging to prepare the ground for the new crops, and raising seedlings on the windowsills, in the spare bedroom, in the airing cupboard, in the greenhouse and in fact anywhere there was a bit of space.

Now that we had the polytunnel things could be started off much earlier, so much so that we even started one crop off on Boxing Day. I had heard that sweet potatoes could be grown in a polytunnel because of the longer growing season, and so we gave it a try. The method was to cut a potato in half and suspend it with the cut side in a glass of water by sticking cocktail sticks in it to support it. The potato grows roots and then shoots appear, which you cut off with a little piece of the potato and again pop into water. When this roots you have your baby sweet potato ready for planting out.

It is a really interesting process and it doesn't stop there. As the plant is a relation to bindweed and a climber you have to provide canes for the runners to scramble up, and yet the crop grows below the ground – a very peculiar plant.

And of course we had loads of chicks running around the place, and in amongst them there were a couple of Coronation boys. As these grew they showed great promise, and eventually fledged into a couple of magnificent cockerels; just what we were waiting for. The genetics of Coronations are complicated, but we needed a good cock bird to mate back to our girls so that we could produce what are known as Splash Coronations. These are basically white birds with odd little patches of colour. The wonderful thing about them is that when Splash hens are mated to a Light Sussex cockerel the resulting offspring are one hundred percent Coronations. Three or four years of selective breeding was finally showing results. The boys had excellent feathering with all the colours in exactly the right places, and were even a pretty good size, which was an added bonus.

Our spring cauliflowers in the polytunnel were wonderful. I had never managed to grow them outdoors so it was truly delightful to have some at last. Served with cheese sauce they were superb and one of my favourite meals. Considering that I hated them as a child this was quite a turn around.

The housing arrangements for the goats were less than ideal, so I decided to put them all together in their original big shed and use the smaller ex-chicken house as a milking parlour. I started by putting *Rosie's* two kids in with *Gertie*. All the kids were much the same size and they had great fun chasing each other around the large pen and playing 'I'm the king of the castle' on the pallets. *Gertie's* boy was promptly nicknamed *'Billy Whizz'* after the comic book character as he was so fast.

If either of *Rosie's* kids went near *Gertie* she waved her horns at them vaguely, warning them off, but there was no real malice. We were doing well so far. But then I brought *Rosie* in and things literally kicked off in all directions as World War Three broke out, with the two adults going at it hammer and tongs, but things took a turn for the worse when they started on the kids, with *Rosie* viciously attacking *Gertie's* baby.

Rosie had clearly discerned that *Gertie* was now weaker after her

difficult kidding, and had decided that she was going to be the
new herd leader. A huge fight ensued with both goats going at
it with clearly serious intentions. I knew by now that goats very
rarely get injured in these fights and that they are really just a trial
of strength. The weaker goat will eventually break away from the
world head butting championships, and that was what happened
here – and it was *Gertie* that backed down for the first time. I
thought that things would settle down now, but oh no. *Rosie* went
after *Gertie* again and again, and then started on *Billy Whizz*,
and *Gertie* then attacked *Rosie's* kids. Things rapidly deteriorated
into a free for all, and when *Billy Whizz* was almost impaled on
Rosie's horns, I knew that the experiment had failed. I quickly
grabbed *Rosie* by the horns and hauled her back to the chicken
shed, rapidly followed by her kids, at least after I had chased them
around the pen a few times before managing to catch them.

A few minutes later, while feeding the chickens, there was a terrific
crash from the direction of the goat pen, followed by several more.
I rushed over to find *Gertie* and *Rosie* battling it out again – with
the steel fence between them! The whole pen shook each time
their heads crashed together.

One of the neighbours now wandered over to see what all the row
was about. I clearly couldn't let the situation continue, but I had
no way of separating the girls any further apart.

When I got the new goat shed I had broken up the old one and
had used sections of it propped against the walls of the sheds to
give the chooks and goats somewhere to shelter from the sun or
the rain. The large roof section was now inside the goat pen with
another section backing onto it in the chicken pen that was now
Rosie's home, so that the area between the two was totally sheltered.
I now had no option but to drag these two sections away from
each other so that they each shielded a section of the steel fencing.
With Rosie's shed door open and pinned back against the wall as

well, it was almost impossible for the goats to see each other and also have sufficient room to rear up and charge. There was only a two foot gap was left and this was the best I could do. Relative peace resumed, with only an occasional crash as one or other of them tried to resume hostilities.

When ducks and geese hatch out, the first living thing that the youngsters see is mum, and they immediately follow her everywhere. This is essential because the mother usually has to lead them straight to water to get them away from predators on land. If you hatch their eggs in an incubator you become mum. We saw this once when we were on holiday when a young lad was running along the seafront, hotly pursued by a young gosling that he had hatched thrashing along behind him, desperate to keep up with its 'mummy.'

Why do I mention this? Well, you may recall that I was the first thing that *Billy Whizz* saw as his head emerged and his eyes opened, but the rest of him was still stuck up *Gertie's* rear end. I think he must have decided there and then that I was daddy: whenever I entered the pen he would come running and jump up at me for attention.

If I sat on the pallets or crouched behind *Gertie* to milk her he would try to climb on my lap. The other two kids now gave me a wide berth, but not *Billy Whizz*, even after he too was given the rubber band treatment. He still loved me and I have to admit that the feeling was mutual as he was such a lovely boy. *Rosie's* kids had short haired auburn coats, but *BW's* was the long haired blonde type that I liked so much. There was clearly going to be a problem in a few months time. I tried to look at him and visualise roasted goat joint, but all I saw was a cuddly and cute little ball of fun.

Any Fool Can Be A.......

Another government con trick

The weather suddenly warmed up and the threat of Bluetongue returned as the midges that spread the disease would now be out and about again.

The government had announced just a few weeks before that vaccine would soon be available to all threatened livestock owners, and that it would only cost one pound to protect each animal. There was widespread relief throughout the smallholding world. Everybody was pleased that the vaccine manufacturers hadn't grabbed the opportunity to make a fast buck with high prices, and the media praised the government for their fast action in ordering enough supplies for everybody.

We were told that we would be allowed to administer the drug ourselves and that we should order our supply through our own vet, which we had done. We couldn't give the vaccine to pregnant goats though, and so we had been forced to wait until after the kiddings. A week after *Billy Whizz* was born the vet rang to say that our vaccine had arrived, and we dashed over to collect it, and sure enough, the vaccine was only one pound a dose.......

.....but there was a snag. In fact there were two, or make that three.It only came in twenty dose bottles, and once the seal was pierced it had to be all used up within three hours. And the label said, 'Do not use on animals less than one month old.' And just to rub it in a second injection had to be given two weeks later.

We now faced a dilemma. Did we start the vaccinations straight away for the two mums, or did we wait until the kids were a month old? The vaccine had been rushed through without having any time to check it for possible effects on young animals. If we started with the mums now, we could include the kids when the second shot was due as they would then be old enough, and then follow that up with second shots for the kids. That would cost sixty quid though, money that we didn't have. Even protecting just the adults, or waiting two weeks for the kids would cost us forty pounds. So much for the 'one pound each to protect your animals' announcements! We found out that some goat keepers were sharing a bottle, dashing around and using it before the three hours was up. The snag was that all those sharing had to be with the same vet, and its use in this way had to be authorised by him. You couldn't just share your bottle with a friend without veterinary supervision, and in any case the only other goat keepers that we knew lived a long way away.

But new Bluetongue cases were being reported on the news, and we knew that we couldn't hold on any longer, so in the end we gave *Gertie* and *Rosie* their shots and vaccinated the under-age kids at the same time. We decided that Bluetongue was such an awful disease, with the animals suffering so badly that we would take the risk of any side effects for the sake of protecting them. All the goats, even the kids, had learned that being tied up was the prelude to something nasty happening, so of course they led us a merry dance round the pens before we managed to secure them.

Jabs were given, and there were no apparent ill effects for the kids and two weeks later we repeated the operation. Our small herd was now protected, but we were forty quid poorer.

I cleaned out *Gertie's* shed and then built a simple milking stand out of pallets and spare timber. Both girls were being absolutely brilliant with milking, although *Rosie's* very small teats made the job a little tricky for my large hands.

We all settled into a steady, if arduous, routine. I would start by milking *Gertie,* leading her into place with a bucket of food. To begin with I tethered her in place, but soon realised that the bucket alone was enough to keep her there, at least until she had eaten everything. I sat behind her and milked her with one hand whilst fending off the attentions of *Billy Whizz* with the other. He soon began to nose around and nibble from mum's bucket though, which made her jumpy, so I was able to distract him with a small bowl of food of his own. *Gertie* would help him to finish it if he ate too slowly. He soon learned to eat quickly.

Their buckets and bowls would be moved outside, with them following, and then *Rosie* would be led in and taken to the milking stand. In typical goat fashion she was interested only in food and could be led from one pen to the other by her nose.

She soon learned the routine and became so good that I could just open her pen door and she would run round and stand by the gate to *Gertie's* pen. As soon as I let her in she would run into the shed, hop up onto the milking stand and wait for her breakfast. As soon as her food was finished she would go looking for a fight with *Gertie,* which signalled that it was time to take her back to her own pen.

I would then turn my attentions to feeding and watering the chickens, collecting eggs, and watering the polytunnel. Watering the tunnel had become somewhat easier as I had set up some effective irrigation systems. I was now writing regularly for two or three magazines and I did regular product reviews for one of them. They would arrange for various companies to send me their products and I would field test them and write about my findings. One month it would be hoes, another spades or forks. One month it was irrigation systems. Brilliant! I now had three different systems set up in the tunnel. As I arrived in the morning I set the hose going to fill the water butt that supplied a drip feed system. By the time I had finished milking the goats the butt would be full (usually overflowing) and I switched the hose to one of the mini sprinkler systems. The whole tunnel was watered whilst I did any other jobs. Of course I could only get away with this because I was on the allotments so early – a notice on the standpipe reads 'Hand held hoses only. No sprinklers.' I could always plead illiteracy, I suppose……

Luckily we didn't have to milk the girls at night. Golden Guernseys produce a lot of milk, but not as much as the big dairy breeds like Saanans or Toggenburgs. By leaving them with the kids who would drink from them throughout the day, we effectively cut out the need for a second milking. Even so, we were still drowning in milk.

Sue had very quickly discovered that the full cream goat milk was too rich for her, and went straight through her system with dire results. She refused to drink any more. On the other hand I loved the stuff and my breakfast cereal became my favourite meal, so much so that I had a bowlful in the evenings too….well *somebody* had to use the milk up!

We made our first attempts at cheese production, and I use the word 'attempts' most carefully. Having read up on the subject we thought it looked simple enough and knocked out our first batch.

'Leave for 30 minutes….cut the curd.'

Hmmmmmm….twenty four hours later we had given up waiting for the curds to form and Sue decided to throw the revolting stuff away whilst I was out working. When she went to do so a couple of hours later – lo and behold – curds were floating in the whey! It produced a strongly flavoured cheese, somewhat drier than the shop-bought cottage cheese usually made from cow's milk. I decided that I would like to try making some garlic and chive cheese, so we chopped up some chives and mixed them in and added one small chopped garlic clove. It didn't seem enough, so I added another clove. When I tried some later in the day Sue could smell it from upstairs.....shall we say that I perhaps overdid the garlic?

The resulting cheese was actually very tasty, but I could still taste it 24 hours later and friends were bginning to give me a wide berth.

Our first batch was made using vegetable rennet and we wondered if this had caused the slow curdling process, so we tried again using lemon juice instead, which worked well with the milk curdling very quickly. We duly hung it in cheesecloth and produced an even drier cottage cheese that looked remarkably like ice cream. It had a strong lemon flavour though, which I didn't like, and so we decided to give it the garlic and chive treatment.

How did it taste? Well, lemon washing up liquid is probably the closest I can come to describing it. In the end we threw it all away.

So it was back to the drawing board. For our third try we reverted to the vegetable rennet, but this time we stirred it briskly after about twelve hours when a skin had formed. It very quickly separated out.

We hung it for about 24 hours and then added chopped chives and just one small garlic clove, finely chopped. The result was fantastic; extremely tasty but not overpowering. So, to mix metaphors, it was a case of patience is a virtue and third time lucky!

I was the only one eating it though, and with all this full fat milk my waistline was spreading, despite the amount of exercise I got.

We were also still throwing a lot of milk away and with the cost of feed, our milk was proving to be very expensive, and we were still buying it in for Sue.

Then we heard that Golden Guernsey flocks in Wales had been found to have Tuberculosis, and that some owners had contracted TB after drinking the unpasteurised milk. I was drinking unpasteurised milk. With Foot and mouth disease, avian influenza, Bluetongue and now tuberculosis – it seemed as though we were living through the biblical plagues. I was expecting to hear of an invasion of locusts on the 6.00 news or an impending sin flood!

And of course the goats continued to make life 'interesting.' *Gertie* and *Rosie* were still attacking each other through the fence whenever the opportunity presented itself with no sign of an imminent truce.

One day, after I had finished the early morning routine and been working in the polytunnel for a while, I heard a bit of a commotion in the goat pen. When I went to investigate, I found *Rosie's* two kids being chased around by *Gertie* – in *Gertie's* pen. After hastily retrieving them and replacing them in their own quarters with a good scolding I checked the fencing. I found a hole about six inches square where the thick steel wires had been snapped by the constant headbutting of the two adults. I went off to rummage in my shed for some wire to make repairs, but by the time I had found some and returned, one of the kids was again being chased around by *Gertie,* and *Billy Whizz* had his head stuck through the gap, trying to push his broad shoulders through to investigate *Rosie's* pen.

I repaired the gap with a crisscross of wire.

A few days later I had to repair another hole. And another. And then another. It brought back odd memories of the polytunnel under siege from the fox and squirrel population with an ever so slightly sour taste of déjà vu.

Checking the fencing became a daily job on top of all the other daily chores. It certainly showed me how much damage a goat's horns could do if they were so inclined. I would be a little more cautious about leaving any tender parts of my anatomy exposed near them after this!

Don't you just love nature?

Our gooseberry crop just disappeared! We were not being careless; one day it was there, with lots of lovely big berries, the next day it was all gone.

It may have been two-legged predators (we had previously lost our butternut crop), or it may have been birds; I've no idea, but at least it was an improvement on the previous year when sawfly caterpillars ate all the leaves in early spring and the bushes didn't produce a crop at all!

We *did* get a lovely crop of redcurrants though, and for once I managed to securely net them and keep the blackbirds, pigeons and other assorted thieves away.

The strawberries were scrummy too, grown beneath a cagework of stiff plastic netting.

Just to give you a brief insight into how idyllic the good life really is, I spent many hours picking cabbage white caterpillars off the Brussels sprouts and other brassicas. There were enough to half fill a two litre ice cream tub, which led me to idly consider a list of the world's least successful ice cream recipes. The netting keeps the birds away, but the butterflies can easily slip through the mesh. It's such a shame the chickens don't eat them – a real waste of protein.

Hugh Fearnley-Whittingstall recently wreaked vengeance upon slugs in his TV programme by cooking and eating them – I think that he should come up with a recipe for cabbage white caterpillars. Baked caterpillar and *gallant soldier* pie for the chooks would work for me!

Holes started to appear in our apples. I don't mean maggot holes, we are used to those, although I really should try to buy some grease bands to wrap round the trunks in autumn. I mean *big* holes. Peck holes. Dirty great *crow* peck holes.

Some mornings when I arrived on the allotments early I caught the damn things perched on the branches pecking away merrily, the small branches bending dangerously under their weight.

I bought a catapult. Not just any old catapult, but a black widow hunting catty that straps onto your arm and is wickedly powerful. I bought a pack of ammo, which is basically small ball bearings. They looked a bit too small to be able to do much damage to a crow so I bought a big bag of marbles at a car boot sale for a quid – they looked *much* more lethal.

Peck holes started to appear in my butternut squashes and pumpkins too. *Big* peck holes so I began to get some target practice, lining up tin cans at the end of the plot and taking pot shots at them. Foxes emerging at dusk became an interesting moving target too. From 200 yards away I couldn't do them much harm, but when a ball bearing hit a shed 2 inches from a fox's nose, its reaction was quite amusing.

The catapult is held firmly in the left hand with a harness attached to the firer's arm for added support and strength. The elastic is pulled right back to nose level using the right arm. It is very similar to the firing position in archery, with your body at right angles to the target. Bearing in mind that I am very tall and consequently have very long arms, that elastic is pulled back a long, long way and has a terrific amount of power when released. The strain on the arm holding the catty is quite considerable...but of course I *didn't* consider it.

I spent two hours practising one evening, knocking seven bells out of the tin cans. It reminded me of most of the westerns I had seen as a kid where the 'greenhorn' had to become a gunslinger to defeat the cattle baron's possee that was terrifying the new settlers, who were perhaps really the downshifters of their day. Anyway, I was becoming quite a deadly shot.

But I woke up the next morning in agony, which I can't remember happening to Jimmy Stewart in any of those westerns! Having previously torn the tendons in my right arm trying to start some machinery, I had now done the same to my left arm playing with a catapult! As luck would have it, it was nowhere near as badly injured as my right arm, but even so it took a couple of months to heal and I was back on light duties as the crows feasted.

A friend suggested that I get a scarecrow, and he gave me the ideal candidate – a stuffed toy in the shape of a truly *huge* American Bald Eagle with outstretched wings. I lashed the eagle's feet to the corner post of the goat pen overlooking the fruit trees, and it looked most impressive. When the wind blew its wings even moved a little. It was visible from way across the allotments too and looked most lifelike.

When I arrived early one morning I found a crow sitting on the fence next to it! Those crows were now taking the Mickey and they had to go – I was gonna get me a real gun!

MIKE HAD THE BIGGEST PECKER...

.....IN HIS SIGHTS!

You may have noticed by now that I tend to bend the allotment regulations a little but sometimes a downshfter's gotta do what a downshifter's gotta do!

So my friend loaned me a powerful airgun, and I took up a concealed position at dusk each evening. The crows tended to gather in the uppermost branches of an oak tree before flying off to roost in a nearby park as the light failed. The branch was very exposed, and the crows were silhouetted nicely. I could creep up quite close, lean the rifle on a low shed and fire up into the tree. I suppose I was firing from fifty feet away. There was a very satisfying thud each time the pellet hit plumage, but all it seemed to do was frighten them into flight and they headed off to the park.

On one occasion I succeeded in knocking one out of a tree and it plummeted downwards, but it managed to regain control just before it hit the ground. By this time they were getting wise to me and they started to fly off to the park as soon as I crept forward, but there did seem to be less of them.

Maybe the lead poisoning was getting them.

They've certainly left my apples alone this year.....but the wasps have moved in instead.

Nature. Don't you just *love* it?

Decisions, decisions

We have always been brutally honest about what hard work it is to raise your own food. Too many people see the whole concept through rose-tinted glasses and think it must be easy to do. Our articles in magazines and indeed our first book "*RaisingChickens for Eggs and Meat*" have, if anything, been aimed at discouraging certain people from getting involved in the *Good Life* by showing them just how bad it can be. "We'd love to grow our own vegetables," is something we've heard so often that it now makes us want to scream!

The truth is that just about anybody can grow some of their own food no matter where they live. A tub on a 27th floor balcony will grow a few lettuces or tomatoes, but I bet the crows will still find them, even up there!

The hardest part will always be the self-sufficiency bit; trying to actually buy very little in the way of foodstuff.

Our quest to achieve this was now entering a crucial stage as we had three kids growing very rapidly - three *male* kids that were effectively unwanted by anybody; three male kids that would eventually have to go to slaughter, with all the trauma that this would involve, and that time was rapidly approaching.

The five goats between them were now eating a prodigious amount of feed. A sack of concentrate that had lasted the two girls a month was now only lasting a week, and the price of that sack had risen steeply too, almost doubling in fact. They goats were now costing us something like £15 a week, and that was just for feed, hay etc. If a proportion of the vet's bills were added it really stacked up. We kept telling ourselves that all these costs weren't just to provide us with milk, but were also there to give us a variation in our meat diet. But of course we had to be able to make ourselves *eat* that meat, and we had to be able to make the trip to the abattoir to produce that meat.

Billy Whizz was becoming more and more tame despite my best attempts to put him off. He was such a cute little rascal that it was very difficult to remain aloof from him.

So now we faced possibly the hardest part of our journey. We had three male kids who were growing fast, and one would soon have to make a one way trip to the abattoir.

We had hoped to be able to load him into a large dog cage placed on plastic sheeting in the back of our estate car, but when I telephoned the slaughterhouse I learnt that this was illegal due to the need to disinfect. Personally I would have thought that the cage and plastic could be disinfected, but it seems that a vigilant officer may have wanted to run a hose inside our family car, so this idea was shelved. We would have to use the trailer which was a great disappointment as we felt that the journey would be much less stressful our way, and animal welfare is after all one of the core reasons why we raise our own. Luckily the abattoir is only about 25 miles away.

The only good news from the phone call was that the cost was going to be much less than we had been led to believe by friends, and the kid would be slaughtered and butchered for £25. Having checked the price of lamb in the butchers, it seemed that our meat would work out at a reasonable price, and more importantly from our point of view, we would know that it had had a good life.

Could we eat the meat though?

So we made the arrangements and booked one of the kids in for the chop in two weeks time.

All three kids were fitted with ear tags which made them ready for their movement to the slaughter house. Under new DEFRA regulations that had came into force a few months earlier, they now had to be double-tagged, which meant that you have to endure their squealing and thrashing about twice – and it was worse with the second ear as they now knew that what you were trying to do was going to hurt!

I sprayed their ears inside and out with an antiseptic to prevent infection, as the ear tags had to be punched right through the ear. All you need to do is load one of the tags into a tool a little like a pair of pliers, position it on both sides of the ear away from the main veins and squeeze hard. It sounds easy enough, but the second you squeeze, the kid rears like a bucking bronco and squeals as though you are murdering him.

I had hoped that doing this to *Billy Whizz* would make him hate me, but not a bit of it – and he actually looked so sweet with his ears dyed blue by the antiseptic, and the lovely bright yellow earrings that were his ear tags, contrasting against them.

I knew that he couldn't be the first one to go, so we chose one of *Rosie's* kids that was usually very stand offish. Her other one was quite friendly, although nowhere near as friendly as *Billy Whizz*.

It didn't really make it any easier, to be honest. The day dawned grey and overcast, and it pretty much reflected my feelings. I took our trailer over to the allotments at 6.00am to avoid having to explain to the other plot holders what was going on. I had already had enough stick from most of them in the weeks leading up to slaughter day, so I really couldn't face more on the day itself. Most of them couldn't understand how we could raise an animal with love and care, and then kill and eat it. My arguments about a happy life and a humane death had fallen on deaf ears – I think that they all believeed that meat is born in joints encased in shrink wrap.

The youngster creatied merry hell from the very second that he was separated from mum and his brother, and had to be dragged across the plots to the waiting trailer. He was made as comfortable as possible, and then I made the 25 mile journey to the abattoir. I had absolutely no idea what to expect, and was as nervous as young billy when we arrived.

A large livestock trailer was being unloaded, backed up against the delivery bay. A large bullock and six sheep emerged, clearly terrified. The bullock was bellowing and thrashing about, and the abattoir workers had a job controlling him. This did not bode well, and my stomach was churning as I approached a chap in a long brown coat who seemed to be in charge.

He was a very pleasant gent, who I realised afterwards must have been the ministry vet. I explained that I had a young goat on a tether in the trailer, and that the trailer didn't have a ramp, so I couldn't back up to the loading bay - could I possibly walk him in? He told me that this wasn't allowed, and so I was made to reverse my trailer between a host of cars and trailers parked all over the place outside the yard, and then turn it ninety degrees into a tight space and back up to their gates. All this with a motley crew of farmers, bystanders and factory workers watching!

Of course I made a complete pig's ear of it, and ended up jack-knifing the trailer across their forecourt, much to the amusement of all concerned. As I drove forward to straighten up there was a sharp crack, and when I checked what had happened I found that by jack-knifing I had driven the two long prongs of the securing padlock clean through the back bumper of my car, and that driving forward had now snapped them off completely, leaving them impaled in the bumper looking like a pair of crossbow bolts.

At this point I got out of my car, opened up the trailer, climbed in and lifted young billy out in my arms. I marched across to the gate and said, "OK, now you know why I didn't want to back in – where do I take him?" and looked the vet in the eye.

It worked. I was now allowed to take him through to the receiving pen in my arms, which in retrospect was actually a bad mistake, as my last memory of the young lad was to see this tiny creature cowering in the corner of an enormous room, absolutely terrified.

I was very upset and barely able to talk to the workers afterwards as we completed all the necessary movement certificate papers and I drove home in tears.

Word obviously went round the place, because when we returned five days later to pick up our meat there was a different atmosphere. The workers in the processing side were very friendly and sympathetic, and assured us that young billy had been left to calm down before being slaughtered, and was happy and relaxed when he met his end. They showed us round the cold store and the sausage-making plant, and we too were happy and relaxed when we left – with 28 pounds of meat! We were really surprised by how much meat we got from the wee lad, and I for one didn't associate this big bag of butchered meat with the lovely kid that I had taken there a few days before.

The following Sunday we had a beautiful roasted shoulder of goat…and eight veg.

On Monday we had cold meat….and eight veg and on Tuesday goat meat pie….and eight veg and on Wednesday minced goat meat and dumplings…and….yes, you get the general picture, don't you. Meat and two veg in our house is simply not an option.

It was the tenderest, tastiest meat that I have ever eaten, without a word of a lie. It simply melted in my mouth, and was very similar to lamb.

Did we feel happy about the whole process?

Actually no, we didn't, is the simple answer. I can kill a nasty, aggressive cockerel with no difficulty, but these lovely creatures with their big trusting eyes and long eyelashes are a different ball game. I was upset on the day that I took the kid to slaughter, but I had no problem eating him. Sue hadn't been so lucky though, and although she had eaten the meat and enjoyed it, she was struggling to come to terms with it all.

We now had two more kids that had to go for the chop soon, and we knew that it would not get any easier.

Any Fool Can Be A.......

Bye bye Gertie

Y ou can buy an awful lot of organic milk for £15 a week!

True, we had also been feeding up three billies for future meat, but we had no allowance in our weekly budget for meat as we have not bought any for 5 or so years. The cost of keeping the goats, taken from our small income, was crippling us.

We also didn't realise that under new laws the vet would have to make a house call every six months in order to prescribe the medicines and vaccines that the girls needed – Bluetongue vaccine too was something else that we had suddenly needed and hadn't budgeted for, and so this was another unplanned expense.

To cap it all, Sue couldn't even drink the milk!

The goats were taking an hour every morning to feed, milk, give fresh hay and water, etc. Other jobs weren't getting done as I struggled to keep on top of everything and also earn enough to pay basic bills by working two days a week in a supermarket.

The horrendous experience of slaughtering our first kid was really just the last straw, but I could not clear the image of the poor lad cowering in the corner of the holding pen from my mind.

Billy Whizz still considered himself to be my best friend and deep in my heart I knew that I just couldn't bring myself to take him to the abattoir, and I certainly couldn't eat the meat afterwards. But I couldn't afford to keep him either – feeding an unproductive mouth was simply out of the question. All our experiences clearly meant that we wouldn't be able to mate the girls again. We were faced with the sad fact that we had no real option but to sell them.

Reluctantly we put them up for sale and advertised them on ACL.

Almost immediately we found a buyer for the girls, as Golden Guernseys are so rare. Due to the high slaughter costs the buyer couldn't afford to pay us anything for the boys though, and would merely take them for free and have them slaughtered later. This would have spared us the ordeal of another trip to the abattoir, but after the high cost of producing and raising them we really couldn't afford to give them away, and as a result we still faced the prospect of taking *Billy Whizz* and his half brother on the one way trip, whilst the girls would head north for a new life.

As the date for the girl's move drew closer we were both becoming more and more anxious about Billy's fate, and I was becoming badly stressed because I knew that we hadn't actually solved the problem – I certainly couldn't take Billy to slaughter. I was becoming like a zombie from lack of sleep.

Out of the blue we received an offer at the last minute from a fresh buyer, who was willing to pay a fair price for all four goats, and she promised to keep *Billy Whizz* as a companion for their own billy. The goats would have 6.5 acres of shrubland to roam around in Sussex. Her granddaughter had an illness that meant she couldn't drink cow's milk. The lady needed to increase the number of goats that she kept to cope with the increased milk needs. She had been around goats all her life and was very experienced. Our lovely girls couldn't have wished for a better home.

We didn't hesitate. Although we felt bad letting our original buyer down, we had no qualms whatsoever as it meant that young Billy would live, and have a good life. Our original buyer obviously wasn't pleased to be let down, but she took it with good grace.

Any Fool Can Be A.......

We eventually heard that she had found a nanny and kid closer to home, and were pleased that it all turned out well in the end.

Our new buyer and her hubby turned up very promptly – probably afraid that we would change our minds again. Their trailer didn't have a loading ramp and was quite high off the ground, so you can imagine the fun and games that we had getting the goats on board. All four had to be lifted in, and old *Gertie* was no lightweight, I can tell you!

The last sight I had of them was four very puzzled sets of eyes looking at me.

So the goats started new lives in Sussex, and judging by the photos that the buyer sent us, they are enjoying a very laidback lifestyle and munching their way steadily through those acres of bushes.

We were very sad to see them go as you can't help but get fond of these lovely creatures, especially with the close personal day to day contact. In all honesty though, we believe that they have a better quality of life in their new home and we consider this to be one of the most important aspects of raising livestock.

The allotments now seemed a sad and lonely place though, and the empty goat shed was a constant reminder. So three weeks later we bought some turkeys.

And Finally

Of course, even keeping a couple of turkeys couldn't pass without some sort of drama. Somebody reported us to the Council for keeping them without permission (probably jealousy, because they wanted to keep turkeys themselves), and we received a letter ordering us to remove them from the allotments. As the letter arrived just two weeks before Christmas we weren't unduly worried.

One of them tasted superb for our Christmas dinner and the other one went into the freezer for a later celebration. Killing them wasn't easy though, as they were such gentle and trusting creatures.

Everybody who raises livestock for the table faces this unpleasant job when an animal reaches maturity and it doesn't get any easier. Why the government in their great wisdom have made it so difficult for a home kill I really don't know.

So many obstacles are now placed in your way. If we could have had the kids slaughtered on the allotments, quietly and in a stress-free situation (for both them and us), we probably would have found a way to keep them, possibly by allowing one of the girls' milk to dry off, thus reducing the feed bill, and mating them alternately.

I would still love to be allowed to keep pigs on the allotments, but it seems a forlorn hope. I believe that buying them as young piglets and raising them to a good size before taking them to slaughter wouldn't be a problem, as they don't have quite the same 'cuteness' factor as young kids or rabbits. I probably won't get the chance to test the theory though.

In the meantime we are drifting towards becoming vegetarian again, or at least vegechookarians. Are we M.A.D. ?

Of course we are. We are Middle-Aged Downshifters, without any doubt.

We have dropped out of the accepted system. We exist on very little income and have almost made a game out of it.

Are we also mad in the true sense of the word? I think we probably are.

Life is a struggle and I now work harder than I ever did when I was a full-time employee. If it is the 'Good Life,' then why is it such hard work?

Will we continue? Of course we will! The taste of our own meat, eggs, fruit and vegetables is far superior to anything we can buy, and we know exactly what has gone into it. And the sense of satisfaction from raising your own food is immense.

We may have to make some changes on the allotments as a lack of time to do all the work because we have to earn an ever-increasing income means that the weeds are often winning the battle for supremacy in our veg patches. We are seriously thinking of putting plastic on our netting tunnel to create a second polytunnel, as tunnels are such good growing environments and you can work in them when the weather outside makes it too bad to venture out. Our big tunnel is usually immaculate inside, even when the outside plots are overgrown.

Some areas on the plots are being 'put to bed' by covering them with tarpaulins. I can't currently manage these areas, and I can't bear to see them become overgrown, but the situation may change in the future, so I don't want to give up any plots....and if we do eventually manage to get a couple of pigs, then the problem would be solved – they would clear the area, dig it and muck it all in one go.

I know that we are getting such good crops from the polytunnel, that with a second one built we may well be able to manage to grow all we need with just two allotments instead of four. If we do convert the net tunnel to a polytunnel, then we will reposition it so that it sits beside our first tunnel. This will be a step towards giving up the top two plots.

Good sense tells me that when we can buy a huge sack of organic potatoes locally for a few quid, there isn't much point in slogging to produce our own, and potatoes would take up such a large part of one of the plots. Some of the fruit trees from the orchard area might be moved to our garden at home, where we can protect them better from the crows, wasps and any two-legged thieves, as well as possibly giving them a bit better attention and care. We are growing our crops in increasingly deeper drought conditions, and we have found that the trees really do need a fair amount of water to bear a decent crop. Sadly they rarely get watered as the orchard is right at the very top of our plots, furthest away from the water supply, and three hoses need to be connected up to reach them. I'm ashamed to say that I rarely have the time or, worse still, don't make the effort when I do. I think that at home they would be less likely to die of thirst.

Perhaps we should plant olive trees on the allotment. Are desert cacti edible I wonder? I've seen them get water from them in films when stranded in the desert, but I don't think there's a need for a water farmer in the UK yet. Although I can foresee a time in the near future when there will be!

We are learning to be crafty, and are now using leaf mould mulches and mulch sheeting to keep the weeds at bay, and as such are cutting down on the amount of time that we have to spend hoeing and hand weeding.

We have discovered worms and wormeries, and the wonderful weed seed-free fertiliser that they produce, which will help us to grow better fruit and vegetables and can also be used as a top dressing that creates fantastic mulch and keeps the weeds down.

Any Fool Can Be A.......

We now have three wormeries running in the back garden and I am building a large one on the allotments. When I have finished this book and sent it off to the publishers, I shall start work on a new book about worms and wormeries. I am convinced that we can all make good use of worms to process our household and garden waste to provide superb compost in which to grow ever better crops.....and at the same time send less waste to the landfill sites, reducing our carbon footprint. Even newspaper and cardboard can now be composted with good effect.

We have found somebody who has horses and we now have access to unlimited amounts of free horse manure to enrich our poor sandy soil – see, that little word 'free' is still popping up. I do so love it. The horse muck will also be used in the large wormery to produce juicy fat worms and lots of wormcast.

We are trying our hand at building up our own small business recycling worn out old 1950s furniture by stripping and painting chests of drawers etc. and fitting them with bun handles for the 'Shabby Chic' look. We sell them through a unit in an antique centre. Early signs are encouraging, and the whole thing fits in well with our green beliefs. We do of course have to find the time to do all the work though, in addition to everything else in our busy lives.

So why are so many downshifters middle aged?

It's quite simple really. We are the only group of people that can *afford* to downshift! Anybody with a mortgage or paying rent would really struggle to make ends meet – we are finding it hard enough without a mortgage. A lot of people aged 50+ not only have no mortgage, but also have a pension income. They are now the only ones who can *really* afford to downshift.

There is an ever-increasing army of us; grey haired men and

women who no longer trust supermarket food, who have turned their backs on what has become the recognised social system. Just a generation ago most people grew a lot of their own fruit and vegetables, but today's youngsters think food only comes in plastic dishes wrapped in cellophane. They have forgotten or never known what real food tastes like.

Thanks to the efforts of people like Hugh Fearnley-Whittingstall large numbers of people are now returning to the old ways – and thankfully they don't all have grey hair!

It's only a short step from growing your own to downshifting. So are you thinking of joining us? If so we'll probably bump into you in the charity shop, or at the car boot sale. And yes, we are *all* mad. But perhaps not quite as mad as everyone else!

The End.....

Unless you are also going M.A.D.......

Also by Mike Woolnough

Raising Chickens
for Eggs and Meat

ISBN 9781904871422

Whether you just fancy your breakfast eggs fresh from the nest box or want to savour a most succulent and tasty roast chicken dinner, made all the more enjoyable because you know that the bird had a good life, this realistc and honest no-nonsense guide will help you to achieve both.

Raising Chickens for Eggs and Meat covers all aspects of looking after chickens, from the joys of seeing your first chicks hatch, caring for them and helping them develop into happy and healthy birds, to seeing them safely and humanely dispatched. It avoids the rose tinted image of keeping chickens and tells it 'how it is,' covering diseases, housing, breeding, security and butchering, together with the everyday joys, making it a realistic book that will ensure that any prospective chicken keeper is fully aware of their responsibilities to their livestock.

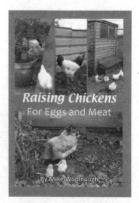

"A genuinely useful and informative book for those keepers looking to maximise the productivity of their birds"
Practical Poultry Magazine

Thinking of Going M.A.D?

The Urban Farmer's Handbook
ISBN 9781904871279
By Paul Peacock

Do you have a yearning to turn over your lawn to grow veg?
Are you finding your talk in the pub turning more to how to
control aphids rather than the latest football transfer?
Have you a desire to go and collect freshly laid eggs, learn how
to tie onions, make sausages or milk a cow?
Do your fantasies these days involve producing an all home-
grown and raised Christmas dinner for the table?

More and more people are seeking a return to a simpler, more self-sufficient
life and digging over their once ornamental lawn to produce veg for the
family, keep chickens for their eggs and meat, make their own cheese, bacon
and jams and even have a pig or a lamb for the freezer.

Paul's book is the perfect springboard for anyone wishing to grab their
own slice of the good life and combining it with urban living. Packed with
practical solutions it will enable you to get the most from your veg bed and
livestock whilst giving you the very best food, the satisfaction of having
achieved it yourself and all the health benefits of a gym membership as you
go about it.

The Good Life Press Ltd.
PO Box 536
Preston
PR2 9ZY
01772 652693

The Good Life Press publishes a wide range of titles for the smallholder, farmer and country dweller as well as **Home Farmer**, the monthly magazine for anyone who wants to grab a slice of the good life whether they live in the country or the city.

Other titles of interest:

A Guide to Traditional Pig Keeping by Carol Harris
An Introduction to Keeping Sheep by J. Upton/D. Soden
Building Fences and Gates by Andy Radford
Build It! by Joe Jacobs
Build It! ..with Pallets by Joe Jacobs
Craft Cider Making by Andrew Lea
Flowerpot Farming by Jayne Neville
Grow and Cook by Brian Tucker
How to Butcher Livestock and Game by Paul Peacock
Making Country Wines, Ales and Cordials by Brian Tucker
Making Jams and Preserves by Diana Sutton
The Bread and Butter Book by Diana Sutton
The Cheese Making Book By Paul Peacock
The Frugal Life By Piper Terrett
The Pocket Guide to Wild Food by Paul Peacock
The Polytunnel Companion by Jayne Neville
Precycle! by Paul Peacock
Raising Chickens for Eggs and Meat by Mike Woolnough
Raising Goats - Meat - Dairy - Fibre by Felicity Stockwell
The Medicine Garden by Rachel Corby
The Sausage Book by Paul Peacock
Showing Sheep by Sue Kendrick
The Smoking and Curing Book by Paul Peacock
The Urban Farmer's Handbook by Paul Peacock

www.goodlifepress.co.uk
www.homefarmer.co.uk

Visit us and become a fan on Facebook

Home Farmer Magazine - the perfect companion for anyone who is M.A.D., going M.A.D. or thinking of going M.A.D.